From Kitchen Sink to

Boardroom Table

From Kitchen Sink to Boardroom Table

Joan Blaney
and
Richard Scase

BLACKAMBER BOOKS

Published in 2003 by
BlackAmber Books
3 Queen Square
London WC1N 3AU
www.blackamber.com

10 9 8 7 6 5 4 3 2 1

A full CIP record for this book is available from the British Library.
ISBN 1–901969–17–7

Typeset in 11/15 pt Optima
by RefineCatch Limited, Bungay, Suffolk
Printed and bound in Finland by WS Bookwell

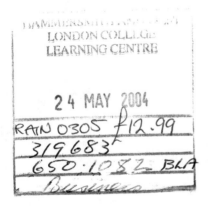

For Joyce Sidhu:
A courageous woman

Acknowledgements

We would both like to thank a number of people:

Joan's dearest friends Alan Cross, for his advice and support, Gurbaksh Johal for her keen observations, Natasha Etti for her helpful contribution, and also Joan's wonderful daughter Siobhan Marie Blaney for her candid critique.

Heartfelt thanks are due from us to all the women for sharing their life stories, knowing that they will be of immense benefit to others.

Contents

Contents

Foreword

This book will be a source of inspiration and encouragement for all women, especially those who have experienced trauma in their personal lives, often at the hands of their partners, and those who have encountered tragedies which ripped their lives apart.

There are two ways to respond to negative experiences like these. Some women choose to give up, to act as a victim and to blame others for the personal grief that has to be borne. This unfortunately only leads to bitterness and often to outright despair. Others choose to stand up and fight, to overcome the odds and to recognise that, ultimately, we are all in charge of our own lives. This book is about exactly those kinds of women.

But it goes further than that. Proof exists to show how the skills that women develop from coping with adversity can be adapted and utilised for their personal advantage in the heart of the business world – the boardroom.

What gives us better money-management skills? Reading a textbook on an MBA programme, or supporting two children when our partner, without any warning, walks out of the door?

In their blinkered obsession with qualifications, companies are over-looking the true business talents that exist among ordinary women in modern Britain. It could be that if employers threw away many of their preconceived ideas about management potential, there would no longer be any of the skill shortages that we hear so much about.

From Kitchen Sink to Boardroom Table contains many important messages for women in all walks of life, women who may, at this moment, be feeling that the odds against them are just too high. However, as this book reveals, this simply is not the case. We women have so much to offer, and the opportunities *are* there.

Baroness Betty Boothroyd, House of Lords
First woman Speaker of the House of Commons 1992–2000

Introduction

We decided to embark on this project after many years of working with women and seeing how they utilise skills that are often under-valued at home, and yet are highly sought-after and marketable in the workplace.

On a daily basis, women across the world plan, organise and deliver an extraordinary range of services to their family and their community, often in isolation and against conditions of intense pressures of money, time and responsibility.

Having heard the notion of women's transferable skills bandied around for years, we wanted to formalise it in a way that we hoped would be of benefit to women, many of whom still lack self-confidence and self-esteem, in spite of all that they have achieved in their lives.

In each chapter of this book we first describe common experiences from which a particular skill emerges – like knowing how to negotiate a deal or to manage conflict.

We then hand over to two women, each of whom relates a vivid and sometimes dramatic narrative of how they came to acquire that skill. Maybe they were born with it, or more commonly were forced to learn it by a sudden change in their circumstances as individuals and as mothers.

Each of these personal accounts is instructive, honest and enlightening.

There follows a short Summary in which we define and analyse what has happened in the women's stories and this continues with brief Self-Help Tips, advising on 'dos and don'ts' to help us avoid the same pitfalls in our efforts to attain our goals.

Finally, we put the women's experiences into terms that relate to modern business skills.

With society moving from a manufacturing and industrial focus to the new softer skills of personal, team and corporate services, the need for female know-how is becoming more apparent and women everywhere should be made aware of this.

This project has been a powerful experience for us, listening to women talk modestly about their achievements, often without realising the life-changing importance of their actions.

Our hope is that this book will help women to recognise the value of their skills and start believing in themselves, as both they and the wider community can, without the shadow of a doubt, profit from this belief.

Joan Blaney
Richard Scase

CHAPTER ONE

MARY AND ANGELA **Overcoming the Odds**

It appears to be in our nature to side with the under-dog – as we watch, hope and sometimes pray for them to succeed. Perhaps this is because their struggle reflects our own desire to defy logic and circumstance in the face of overwhelming difficulties.

People often say that life is what you make it, and although we may endeavour to make it as easy as we can for our families and ourselves, fate has a way of intervening without warning, and sometimes without mercy, making our lives a misery and replacing our hopes with fears and our happiness with grief.

From a relatively peaceful position you may suddenly find yourself embattled for being in the wrong place at the wrong time, or for having said yes when you should probably have said no.

Whatever the circumstances, if you are lucky to have friends and family around you, you may look to them for support – yet whilst they may give without question, you know that it is up to you to face the obstacles ahead.

At first this may seem a daunting task, but in tackling the unknown you grow in strength and courage, and as you get used to treading the path of danger not even the disappointments or the pain can foil your determination to succeed.

How would *you* face up to the challenges that life can unexpectedly lay before you?

MARY'S STORY

I was the oldest of three children born into an Irish-Catholic family and brought up in Manchester, in the north of England. My brother Ryan and sister Colette and I all went to the local Catholic schools and whilst they were both academically minded, I was more interested in sports.

I was good at gymnastics, hockey and swimming and represented my school and county in all three. My parents were proud of me and bought a special cabinet for all the plaques, trophies and medals that I had won since I was about four years old. My PE teacher used to encourage me and would often say that I was good enough to represent England in any of the three sports as long as I was prepared to work hard.

I did work hard – but that was up until the age of fourteen when I got to the third year at secondary school and then I just lost interest.

It was about the same time that I started to smoke. A lot of my friends already did and were part of the 'smokers' group' who would congregate at break times in the 'smokers' corner, an area behind an old shed at the top of the playground. No one was allowed to join the group unless they also smoked and so, not wanting to be left out, I tried a cigarette. I choked and spluttered at first, and everyone laughed at me, but I had no problems after that and was accepted into the group. Before I knew it, I was spending most of my pocket-money on cigarettes.

My schoolwork took a real dive, and my parents were very angry with me when I was suspended for two weeks for throwing a piece of rubber that bounced off the blackboard and hit the maths teacher on his head. Other pupils had been throwing things too, but I was the only one to hit him.

Following a stern lecture from my dad, I started to concentrate on my schoolwork again and left school with five good GCSE grades in English, Maths, Geography, History and Art.

Although I had lost my desire to compete, I was still interested in sports and went to college on a one-year course to train as a sports and fitness instructor. When I passed I got a job at a local sports centre.

I enjoyed my work, and within months had built up some good clients. But my life took a turn for the worse when an innocent night out with a friend landed me in trouble with the police.

I was in a nightclub and having a good time when a girl I had never seen before came over and started shouting abuse at me. I told her that she was mistaking me for someone else but she wouldn't listen. Not wanting any trouble, I decided to leave the club with my friend, Linda, but the girl and two others followed us outside. I realised things were getting serious when she started coming after me with a glass. As Linda and I were trying to get away, someone grabbed Linda's handbag from her shoulder and along with her make-up, purse and a few other things, a penknife fell out of the bag and onto the pavement. I picked up the knife and before I could get hold of myself, I slashed the girl across her arm. Blood poured from the wound and she collapsed on the pavement. The ambulance came for her and the police car came for me.

I was charged with grievous bodily harm and sentenced to a year in jail. It could have been four, I was told, but the judge showed some leniency because I was only seventeen years old and he accepted that I had been provoked.

Prison was a living nightmare. I kept crying all the time, lost weight because I couldn't eat the food, and being in solitary confinement for hours on end left me traumatised. The only time I felt at ease was when Linda or my parents came to visit.

Drugs were constantly being passed around, and women who hadn't touched drugs until they came into prison were going out as addicts. I never took drugs but I smoked a lot and was often looking to swap phone cards or whatever I could for cigarettes.

I only served six of my twelve months' sentence and when I got out, it took me almost as long to get back to normal. Everything around me was strange, and although I was back home and my family were all very supportive, sometimes I didn't know where I was or where I belonged. On a few occasions when things got really bad, I woke up in my bedroom at home thinking I was still in prison and that there were bars on my bedroom window.

Having lost my job at the sports centre, I was desperate for another one and began working in a packing warehouse. The money wasn't as much as I had been used to, but the work was clean and I met some good people. I stayed there for about two years.

During this time I had caught up with old friends, was going out a lot and met Ricki, who was my first serious boyfriend, at a rave club. He was tall and very good-looking; we had a lot of fun together, but eight months into the relationship he started to become very possessive. We argued a lot and then he began to knock me about and stopped me seeing my friends. He used to take drugs and would bully me into taking some with him. I became very depressed and lost a lot of confidence in myself.

I got the sack from the warehouse and a few other jobs as well because he used to turn up and make scenes and drag me from my workplace. I tried to finish the relationship several times and in the end took out an injunction against him. But this simply made things worse when he managed to break into my flat, held me hostage and threatened to kill me.

He raped me twice during the night and I felt so dirty that I sat and cried in the bath for hours until the water went stone cold. By morning I was deeply distressed and desperate to get away from him. People were passing my window and I tried to get their attention by waving but no one responded. Eventually I pleaded with him to let me get something from the shop, and he said he would let me go if I promised to come back.

I started to sweet-talk him and not only promised to come back but told him that I loved him and wanted to stay with him. He fell for it and as soon as I got through the door I ran as fast as I could to the shop, and then called the police. By the time they and my family got to the flat, Ricki had gone.

It was now that I entered the worst period of my life. Even prison did not come close to this. After the Ricki episode, I was left damaged and addicted, and was soon on every hard drug on the market –

heroin, crack, cocaine, you name it. I lost my flat and my friends, except Linda, although I rarely saw her, and, too ashamed of myself to go home to my parents, I began living on the streets with other addicts. I hung around with a girl named Susie, who was a prostitute and would use the money she made to buy drugs. I never did that but I robbed people, including my own family, to get cash for drugs. I would even trick lorry drivers by pretending to be a prostitute, robbing them as they got ready for action and then running away with the money. I did this a lot, sometimes making up hard-luck stories and pretending to be in distress. When the police finally caught up with me I was arrested and spent another two months in jail.

It was dangerous being on the streets because there were a lot of people on crack who were paranoid and could be friends with you one moment and hold a knife to your throat the next. But I felt no fear because I, too, was high on crack most of the time and would live in crack-houses with different people, sometimes not even knowing who they were.

Women were often raped, and when this happened to me and I went to the police, they didn't even bother to take a statement because I was a drug addict on the streets and deserved whatever I got.

I lost even more of myself after that; I wasn't washing or eating, went down to seven stones from ten, and seldom knew what day it was.

But I was conscious that people were dying around me. One choked on his vomit whilst he was asleep, a couple were shot, and others stabbed to death. I still don't know how I did it, but I managed to pick myself up and go home to my parents. I knew that I was in a real state from the expression on my mother's face when she opened the door and saw me, and I was crying as I told her that I wanted to come off the drugs but needed help because I couldn't do it on my own. She hugged me and cried as she ushered me through the door.

After I got cleaned up my father took me to a drugs unit and I was put on a rehabilitation programme, which meant that I had to stay at home, and could not leave the house unless it was with my father or Linda.

It was a very difficult time for my family, especially when I started to have withdrawal symptoms. I suffered from aching joints, snapped at people for no apparent reason, and had mood swings where I would either be screaming angrily at my mother or sister, who was still at home, or not speaking to them at all. This had a devastating effect on my mother and caused her a lot of stress, but she was more concerned about getting me off the drugs and kept telling me that everything would be all right.

I experienced ups and downs and bouts of depression for about four months before I started to feel better, and whenever I got the urge to take drugs I would have a small glass of whiskey instead.

Crack had caused me to blank many things from my mind, but now I was getting clean I was haunted by all that had happened to me, and this kept me awake at nights.

I would sometimes get feelings of being dirty, and no matter what time it was, I would get out of bed and start cleaning the house. I would scrub the kitchen floor, wipe down the work surface, clean the toilet and the bath, and used a lot of bleach so that I could smell that everything was disinfected.

After about six months, I was eventually allowed out on my own and although I promised my parents to stay off drugs, I dabbled two or three times and felt guilty afterwards. But I was still weak and kept running into people who knew me and were tempting me to go back on drugs. I would tell them that I was clean but they would say, 'You will never be clean,' and continue to offer me drugs. The last time I dabbled I felt no effect at all, and that was when I really knew that I was finally recovering from my addiction.

It was at least eighteen months before I was properly back on my feet again and started to think about getting myself a job. At first I thought I wouldn't be able to do much more than a cleaning job because my mind was messed up and I was low in self-confidence. But deep down I knew that I was capable of more and that it wasn't too late for me to learn something new.

Because I had a police record, there were some jobs – like being a nurse or working with children – that I couldn't even consider, and it made me sad to think how I had limited my choices in life. But wanting to do something useful, and to be someone, I sat down one evening and made a list of the things I was interested in and enjoyed doing. I loved driving and it was then that the idea of being a Driving Instructor came to mind.

I went to find out about training and when I was told that it would cost three thousand pounds to do the college course, I didn't flinch but set about raising the money. I did any job that came my way – cleaning, bar work, waitressing – and my parents, who could see that I was well and truly back on track and was trying to help myself, also made a contribution towards the cost.

When I first started at the college I was paranoid because, as far as I knew, everyone else on the course had come from a good background; they had never drunk, or smoked, had never been a drug addict and certainly had never been to prison. I felt like the odd one out, and even though no one could have possibly known about me, I kept thinking that they did. It was a long personal battle, trying to keep all those negative thoughts out of my head, but eventually I did, and began to socialise with a few people after classes.

It was two years of solid hard work and sometimes I was up studying till the early hours of the morning, but I kept going and was thrilled when I passed my exams first time. I then went on to take my Advanced Driving Test. This too was hard going, but once again I got through it.

Almost three years after I made my decision to become a Driving Instructor, I got a job with a leading driving school and took my first pupil out on a circuit. I have had quite a few since then who have passed their test and it feels good to know that I taught them to drive safely.

I continue to develop my career and hope one day to become an examiner and to run my own driving school. But for now I will content myself with the fact that I am buying my own house, I have a good and well- paid job, and I am on the way to achieving the goal I set myself in life.

At one time I did think that there was no way out for people like me, and that once you hit rock bottom, like I did, that was it. But now I think differently. There is always something you can do, and always someone there to help you. But more importantly, you have to want to help yourself.

After five years of being clean, I am still haunted by the experiences of my drug addiction and the relationship I had with Ricki. I have been to hell and back, and to see where I am now makes me feel proud of myself.

ANGELA'S STORY

When Mal and I were offered a new life in Jamaica, we jumped at the idea. He was heir to a lucrative hardware business his parents had set up, and they wanted to show him the trade in the run-up to their retirement. The thought that such an opportunity would be fraught with danger for my sons and myself never once crossed my mind.

I had first met Mal fifteen years ago – a couple of months before he was due to emigrate to Jamaica with his parents, Frank and Ruby Harrison. It was love at first sight, and after only a few days, he decided to stay in England so that we could get married. Although his parents were less than happy with his decision, they were supportive and sold us their old house at a very reasonable price.

I already had a son, Jamal, from a previous relationship. Mal took him as his own child, and five years after our marriage we had another son, Thomas. With nine years of married bliss, two wonderful sons, a house and two cars, we were doing well for ourselves, but this was all about to change when we got a call from Mal's parents offering us the chance to join them.

Although we both had well-paid jobs, a lot of firms, including our own, were having difficulties, and the threat of redundancy was looming. Having weighed up the pros and cons, we took voluntary redundancies, sold up and within months were living in the parish of St Anne, which is on the north coast of Jamaica.

It was all too perfect, and sure enough the cracks began to show when I asked about the legalities around the handover of the business and the properties that went with it. After brushing off my curiosity for as long as they could, Mal's parents eventually admitted that it would be a good few years before they even contemplated retirement. On hearing this, Mal and I knew immediately that we had been duped.

Having used our redundancy money and the money we got from the sale of the house to buy trucks for the business and for paying to ship over most of our things, we had very little left to spend on ourselves. They may have thought they were being helpful, but I was outraged when Mal's parents took it upon themselves to decide how much money we needed to get by on and gave him what they called 'pocket-money' for both of us.

Fed up with their patronising behaviour, I told Mal that he had to do something about it but he sided with them, saying we should be grateful for all they were doing for us; he promised that things would get better. But they didn't and I was feeling increasingly trapped.

It was eighteen months before I finally admitted to myself that I longed for our days back in England when we were a real family and the boys were much happier.

Suddenly, one morning, Mal's parents announced that while they could support me, Mal and Thomas, they could no longer afford to look after Jamal and that it would help if he went back to England. I was livid and said no because I was not going to let anyone break up our family. But once again Mal acceded and I had to go along with their suggestions.

I was at home with my parents for three weeks after returning to England with Jamal, and having decided that I would not be staying in Jamaica without Jamal, I promised him and myself that my only reason for going back was to bring Thomas home.

Having got rid of Jamal, Mal's parents were overwhelmingly generous with their gifts and support, as they were when we first arrived in Jamaica. But the only thing I was really looking forward to was returning to England with Thomas. When I told him, Mal said that would not be possible, but knowing that anything was possible as far as my children were concerned, I started on a plan to get Thomas and myself out of the country.

In those days I used to take my clothes to the local launderette and would sit talking with Marva, the woman in charge, and a few other women, whilst the clothes were being washed. Marva supported me in my desire to return to England and one day, after I had come up with my plan, I took a large suitcase of clothes up to the launderette; these were not for washing but for taking with me when I escaped back to England with Thomas.

The next thing I had to do was find a way of getting Thomas to myself long enough for us to get away. Up until that time I was hardly alone with my son. Mal's parents would take him to school in the morning and pick him up in the afternoon and take him to the shop. The only time I was alone with him was during the evenings when the whole family came home.

Then one Wednesday evening, after Mal's mother Ruby said there was no school for Thomas the next day and he would have to stay at home with me, my heart raced, because I knew that Thursday had to be the day.

I called Marva and she arranged for her cousin, who was a taxi driver, to pick me up at midday when I felt certain that the coast would be clear.

That night, I sat down and wrote a very long letter to Mal, telling him how unhappy I was about things, how heartbroken I was to be without Jamal, and how it felt as if we no longer had any control over our own lives. I ended my letter by saying that I still loved him and hoped that he would join us back in England.

By morning I was a nervous wreck, thinking that if I got caught I would have lost the only chance I had to get away with our son. But I kept telling myself that I had to go for it because there was no other way.

It seemed that things would indeed work out when the taxi turned up on the corner of the street as planned, and Thomas and I were soon on our way to stay with friends of my parents in Portland, a good four hours away.

When I rang my parents and told them that Thomas and I were safe, my mother kept telling me to be careful and to get off the Island quickly, but there were problems around the availability of flights and it took us a week to get one.

As we stood in the long queue waiting to check in, I held Thomas as close to me as I possibly could, but within seconds of letting go of him to hand over our tickets and passports, the tall figure of my husband appeared beside me. The next thing I knew, Mal had picked up Thomas and was running away with him.

My bags went flying as I ran after him, shouting, 'Stop!' and screaming, 'That man has got my son!' People turned around but did nothing, and minutes later a car was speeding away with Thomas looking at me from the rear window.

Mal's parents had paid someone to check the names of people who were flying from Kingston to England, and he and a few others had been waiting for us at the airport.

I was devastated and collapsed in despair. Knowing that my ticket was valid to fly out at any time, I went back to Portland and contacted my parents, who advised me to take the next flight home.

When I arrived at Gatwick, having cried throughout the whole nine-hour flight, I expected to fall into the arms of my parents, but it was my elder brother, Winston, who was waiting for me. He held me and simply said, 'Don't worry, Sis. Just think that Thomas is on holiday and will soon be home.' My family had already come up with another plan.

Within weeks of arriving back in England, my parents and I went to get legal advice about taking custody of Thomas. After being told that we would have to appoint a lawyer in Jamaica and that there was no guarantee that Mal or his parents would turn up in court, we decided to take action ourselves. Our solicitor warned us against this, saying that kidnapping was a serious offence, that I could expect a heavy jail sentence and, on top of all that, Thomas could be sent back to Jamaica. But once again, there was no other option and so we had to go for it.

Winston had decided to go back with me to get Thomas, and whilst we were raising the £1,600 needed for our tickets, I kept phoning Jamaica and was gravely distressed when Mal's parents would not allow me to speak to Thomas, not even on his birthday. But I was able to speak to Marva and she kept me up to date with what was going on.

I kept most things to myself because if my mother knew that Mal had made a bonfire and had burned all my clothes, and that his extended family, who were linked to drug dealing and mafia activities, were out to get me, they would have told Winston and me to call off the trip and I would probably never have seen Thomas again.

I felt as if I was embarking on a military operation when I eventually bought the tickets, especially as we were taking an indirect route, which would mean a short stopover in Miami. This, we felt, would make it more difficult for Mal's parents to trace us as they had done before. As I stood outside the travel agency with the tickets in my hands, I said a little prayer, asking God to help us to win through.

Winston, who had left Jamaica as a child and had not been back for almost thirty years, decided that he wanted a chance to tour the island and we did so for a few days. I travelled under my maiden name, and with braided hair as opposed to the short style I normally had. Even so, I wore sunglasses for most of the time because the Harrisons were known in many places and there was a risk that I could be recognised.

On the morning we planned to get Thomas, we set off early from Portland and arrived in St Anne at around seven o'clock in the morning. We parked where we had full sight of the Harrisons' shop and waited for them to arrive with Thomas.

The plan we had made from home was to follow whoever it was who was taking Thomas to school, wait for him to be dropped off and then take him out of the school. But on the morning when we were leaving for the airport, a letter had arrived from Marva with the devastating news that Thomas was no longer going to school. I kept this to myself because, once again, I feared that if my parents knew, they would tell us to call off the trip. As long as we got to Jamaica, I was determined to find a way to get my son – and from what Marva wrote, it would probably be from the shop, which was going to make it harder and more dangerous to seize him.

The shop usually opened at 8.30 a.m. but the Harrisons were late and as time ticked by, I was becoming more and more anxious about what could have happened to them. When they did eventually arrive, it was only Mal and his parents and there was no sign of Thomas.

I was beside myself as I thought that they had sent him away and I had absolutely no way of knowing where he was. But Winston remained calm and said we would start by going to the Harrisons' home; and if I saw Thomas in the garden or anywhere outside the house, I was to grab him and take a taxi back to the airport. Winston had been a heavyweight boxer and felt sure that he would be able to deal with any opposition.

We arrived at the house but could see no one except, by a stroke of luck, Marva. The hired car we were driving had tinted windows and as I wound down the window and Marva recognised me, she started crying and said, 'Miss Angela, you've come back for your son.' I told her that I had and desperately needed to know where he was.

After she told me that it was the first morning that Thomas had been allowed to go back to school, Winston and I were relieved, and reverted to our original plan. Explaining that I had no time to lose, I thanked Marva and we sped on to the school.

The head teacher was pleased to see me when I arrived, but became anxious when I told her that I had come for Thomas. She then explained to me that the Harrisons had threatened to kill her if she allowed anyone, other than themselves, to take Thomas out of school.

Surprised at how calm I was, I simply said that all she needed to say was that I had told her that I had moved back to the house and, knowing that Thomas suffered from mosquito bites, I was taking him to the doctor.

Not waiting for a response, I then stepped past her to look for my son. It was morning break-time and the playground was full of well over 100 boisterous children running around the place. I couldn't see Thomas, and as I stood desperately searching for him, I felt a little hand in mine and heard a voice saying, 'Mummy.' I bent down, swooped him up immediately and made a dash for the car.

Knowing that time was against us, what would normally have been a two-hour journey back to Kingston took us half that time.

But when we got to the airport, the guard checked our tickets and said that although Thomas's ticket was still valid for him to travel, which we already knew, it would only be direct to England as there was no guarantee of a seat for him in Miami.

My heart sank. Gripped by sheer panic, the immense tension of the last few hours and fearful of what might happen this time if we were caught, I broke down in tears and pleaded with the guard to let us through. I told him there was every possibility that gunmen were on their way to the airport and would be prepared to do anything they felt was necessary to take my son away from me.

I don't know quite how much he believed of my story, but after a short while and no doubt a little soul-searching on his part, he agreed to let us through and took us to the front of the queue.

The guard in Miami was also unhelpful at first, but after I repeated my story and explained that on the next flight in from Kingston there could be gunmen after my son and me, she relented and got Thomas a seat on the flight back to England.

It wasn't until the plane took off from Miami that I could finally relax. Thinking back to what my lawyer had said, I knew that there would be difficult times ahead, but even that could not dent the tremendous joy I felt having my son at my side once more, and knowing that his uncle and I were, at last, taking him home.

SUMMARY

Mary and Angela tell very different stories. They describe how experiences like theirs, of hardship (for Mary) and of privilege (for Angela) can lead to crises that can only be overcome with determination.

In Mary's case, we can see how a minor occurrence, or even a simple coincidence, can dramatically change our lives. Everything is quite normal for her until a chance encounter changes everything. She finds herself embroiled in a fight and, in a panic, picks up a knife. Before she knows what has happened she finds herself in jail. After that, it is downhill all the way. She gets involved in a violent relationship from which she is later able to escape, only to become a drug addict thanks to her low self-esteem.

Through her own determination she overcomes the odds. But she cannot do this alone. She has the courage to return to her parents, to resist the temptation of a retreat into drugs and to recognise that she must exercise the greatest willpower.

Her story tells how we can easily become victims of circumstances. These can appear to conspire against us and put us on a downward spiral. But it also shows how we are never, ever *truly* victims. There is always, somehow, a way out. This demands that we have to face up to the facts of life, never reject those who support us the most, and remain determined to break out of the cycle of despair.

For Angela, the circumstances are quite different although, like Mary, she gets into a position where she is temporarily unable to control her own life. Her partner dictates to her how she should lead her life. She is treated as an agent for what *he* wants to do. Her wishes and needs are disregarded. If Mary suffers both physical and emotional abuse, for Angela it is almost entirely the latter. For many women, this can be just as painful.

Angela's story emphasises the need to have a personal strategy to overcome the odds. Her financial advantages, unlike Mary, give her time and space to plan that strategy. But her story also illustrates the importance of staying cool – particularly when the best-prepared strategies start to go wrong. Then there is no substitute for quick thinking, going for the best chance and overcoming whatever obstacles are put in our way.

SELF-HELP TIPS

- Never see ourselves as victims. In every situation there are opportunities to put ourselves in charge – even against the toughest odds.

- To overcome the odds, we have to work out our own personal strategies. For this, we need to know the end of the journey – where we want to get to.

- Nobody is an island. We can hardly ever achieve our ends entirely alone. We usually need the help and advice of others.

- Never take others for granted. On the way down in life we meet those we knew on the way up.

- Seize the opportunities as they arise. Even the best strategies fail to predict what is likely to crop up. It means we always have to be flexible and pragmatic in our solutions.

- Be imaginative and resourceful in problem-solving. As individuals we have distinctive characteristics. These give us personal strengths and weaknesses. We need to know what they are. From our understanding of them, we can develop the imaginative strategies to overcome what, at the time, appear to be impossible odds.

IN THE CORPORATION

It is tough in any modern business. Everything seems to be just fine as we work our way up the corporate ladder. Then suddenly something unexpected happens. We get demoted, lose our jobs, are by-passed for promotion.

Success in the modern corporation is built on self-confidence. On overcoming the odds. The experiences of these two women have given them the strength of character to succeed in spite of the difficulties they faced. And that is the way we have to treat life in the modern organisation. It is a matter of fighting against the odds. Often this means breaking down boundaries, prejudices and preconceived notions against which we are perceived to be unsuitable for promotion to the boardroom. We have two choices: to be victims of the system and plead for sympathy, or to take on anything that stands in our way. The willpower and self-reliance of Mary and Angela show how the odds against us can be turned to our own advantage and can lead us right into the corporate boardroom.

CHAPTER TWO

CRISTIANA AND KAREN Negotiating for Themselves

How often do you find yourself agreeing to do something you don't really want to do, if only to keep the peace? And how many times have you 'made do' with what you've been given because someone hasn't fully understood your needs, and you haven't had the confidence or the opportunity to express them?

Some people will cite increased assertiveness as the answer, but although there is an abundance of books on the subject, many 'assertive' women we know still find it difficult to say, 'No,' to friends and families, and end up feeling angry and upset with themselves for having given in when a good compromise might have been better.

Management Consultants will tell you about the importance of getting to a 'Win Win' position when faced with complex situations at work, and urge you to negotiate so that you can reach a favourable compromise.

But just how do you negotiate for a 'Win Win' position with a headstrong and precocious seven-year-old, particularly after her father has left the relationship and you are feeling as guilty as hell about not being able to make up for the loss? Or, more sensationally, with a husband who is angry about your relationship with another man?

CRISTIANA'S STORY

I met John at a peace rally in London. It was in the heady days of the 1960s a time when people felt they could change things. We were part of a team that organised marshalling and banners, and we fell in love almost immediately. A few months later we got married. It was impulsive but right because, apart from the physical attraction, we had similar interests and shared the same political views.

We both continued our work as committed community activists and were involved in civic action groups. It was during one of these meetings that I met Rodney, who had recently moved into the area and wanted to know more about the neighbourhood. He was tall and good-looking, and I felt uneasy the moment I realised that he was making his way towards me. But we got on extremely well and I was more than happy to tell him about some of the activities the group had been involved in. Even though John and I had been happily married for almost three years, I was instantly attracted to Rodney, who had stirred something in me.

A group of us often went for a drink after our meetings, and one night when John had decided not to join us Rodney and I found ourselves alone together after everyone else had left. It was then that he explained how he felt about me, and said that he wanted to have an affair.

Although I was flattered I was also taken aback by his straightforward approach.

As I pondered the possibility of an affair, I remembered my upbringing in a little village in Spain where, as women, we were not encouraged to think for, or to value, ourselves. Instead we were expected to be domesticated, remain a virgin until we got married, allow our fathers to choose our husbands and only leave home to get married and have lots of children. This way of doing things had made me rebellious and strongly opposed to conventional relationships. A relationship with both John and Rodney would be anything but conventional.

I had not consciously set out to fall in love with any other man, but it appeared to have happened. From my early teenage years I was used to thinking for myself and listening to my own conscience, and so I concluded that there was nothing wrong with what I was feeling.

Rodney took every opportunity he had to flirt with me, and after a few weeks I decided to go along with the affair. It wasn't an easy decision and I thought long and hard about how it would affect my marriage.

Neither John nor I wanted to have children, and well before we got married we had agreed that our relationship would be one that was equal and free. But we had not talked about sexual freedom. Nonetheless, as we had always been open and honest with each other I felt sure that it was worth taking a calculated risk in telling John what I was going to do.

As I got ready to raise the subject with him, I was so nervous that I almost changed my mind. John was a good man, and although I didn't want to lose him neither did I want to deceive him.

When the time felt right, I went ahead and told him, and although the words didn't come out as I had planned, he was left in no doubt about my intentions. Understandably, he was very angry and upset. We argued and he threatened to leave. I waited for things to calm down and then managed to get him to agree to at least allow me to explain exactly how I was feeling.

It was hard work and very emotional, but in the end I was able to convince John that I loved him, and that I was not looking for something he could not give me. Rodney was simply different and that was what I found most attractive about him.

The days that followed were very difficult, but we took time to talk about our needs, our feelings and how important it was for us to live our lives the way we wanted to.

There was little doubt in my mind that I wanted to spend some of my time with Rodney; I simply had to find a way to manage that time and to make sure that it did not impinge too much on my marriage. I know this may sound surreal, but I was certain of my love for these two men and knew that I could make it work for all of us.

After prolonged discussions about our feelings, what we meant to each other and how much we would both lose through a separation, John and I eventually decided on an 'open' marriage that would allow both of us, with discretion, to have relationships with other people.

This was what I had hoped for, but despite the concession John still felt hurt by the whole situation and it was weeks before he finally accepted the relationship I was having with Rodney.

For the first few months, Rodney and I would meet in the early evenings; we went out for meals, had hours of intimate discussions and were free to enjoy each other's company.

I never spoke with John about what we did together, and the only tension arose when I decided to spend the odd night with Rodney.

When I came back in the mornings, or sometimes after work in the evenings, John would be very withdrawn and would hardly speak to me. I learned to deal with this by busying myself with the house-work, suggesting that we did things together, knowing that in his anguish he would probably refuse to, and staying in on my own, even if he had decided to go out without me. It was my way of proving to him that, apart from the extra time I spent away from him, little else had changed and we still had a life together.

We had all been living in Manchester, and after about a year had settled into a comfortable routine until Rodney was promoted and had to move to London to take up his new position. This meant that I was spending longer periods away, often at weekends.

I think this might have been what drove John to turn the tables on me.

My best friend Carole used to spend a lot of time with us but I never thought that John was at all interested in her until he told me that they were sleeping together. I was shocked, and my pontificating to John about how society had conditioned us to feel jealous, and that we had the ability to rise above it, was no help to me at all.

I had this mental vision of a Utopia where people were able to relate to each other with love, understanding and respect, but had no need to own them. To me, jealousy was a sign of ownership and, although it was hard, I was determined not to give in to it.

But more than anything else, I was able to understand how John had been feeling on the nights that I was away with Rodney. It was dreadful, lying alone in bed knowing that he was with Carole, and I realised that it wasn't the *idea* of him being with someone else that was most hurtful, but the *reality*.

Throughout the relationship with John, Carole and I remained friends. She continued to visit our home and we socialised amongst ourselves and with others. On the other hand, I only ever saw Rodney on my own because it would have been naive to think that he and John could have developed a friendship.

After almost a year, John and Carole ended their relationship. John spoke little about what had happened and I was careful not to pry. Instead I was glad to be able to comfort and support him through what were difficult, and quite possibly lonely, times.

I continued to see Rodney because, whilst I had not purposely been looking for multiple relationships, being able to love both John and Rodney was more than I could have wished for.

But my happiness was cut short when, perhaps in despair at having broken up with Carole, John said that he wanted me to end the relationship with Rodney. He then went on to say that he had never been comfortable with the arrangement but had agreed to it because he didn't want to lose me. Furthermore, he had not expected that my relationship with Rodney, which was approaching three years, would have lasted that long.

These were very trying times because I knew that if I agreed to stop seeing Rodney I would only be doing what John wanted me to do, and not making the choice for myself.

At the end of the day, the question was: to whom was I responsible – to John or to myself? This is a question we as women constantly have to answer, and we do so by putting our children, parents, our husbands, and other people first. We look after them and we support them, often to the detriment of our own feelings and ourselves.

Knowing and having accepted my feelings, I knew that if I were to stop seeing Rodney, I would not only be unhappy, but my relationship with John would suffer. Nonetheless, it was not hard to see how hurt John was by the whole situation and that was heartbreaking for me.

Either the three of us would have to find a way of living together, and I would be able to continue to split my time between the two, or I would have to give one of them up.

I knew deep down that the simplest thing to do, for all our sakes, was for me to stop seeing Rodney. But even if I promised to do this, the chances were that I wouldn't stick to it, and would soon be embroiled in exactly the kind of deceit I had been trying hard to avoid. I also knew that if I told Rodney that I had to stop seeing him, he would be devastated and I didn't want that to happen either.

It was at this time that I started to think about what both of these men actually meant to me.

When John and I were together it was like being with myself. He understood me, our minds worked in a similar way and we rarely needed to challenge each other. We were, in every sense, soulmates. On the other hand Rodney, who was a few years younger than both John and myself, was more challenging in our relationship. Lovemaking was also different. John was more affectionate and gentle whilst Rodney was more passionate and exciting.

The more I thought about it, the more I knew that I did not want to stop seeing Rodney. I told John of my decision and explained my feelings to him as I had done numerous times before. But this time, he didn't want to hear them because he had made up his mind to leave.

For his part, Rodney didn't like to see how torn I was between him and John, but nor did he pressurise me into making a decision. He had on previous occasions suggested that I left John to be with him, but had learned to accept that I had no intention of doing that. In time, I think he had satisfied himself with the thought that if John ever left me it would present the perfect opportunity for us to be together.

Throughout the difficult times, it never occurred to me that Rodney would want to leave the relationship, but if he had done my life would still have been perfectly happy, although it would have been different.

John started to make plans to leave and, even though I didn't try to stop him, I made sure that he knew that I still loved him and wanted to be with him.

But there was still a chance for us when he asked if I would agree to see less of Rodney. Although he didn't say it, I knew that he was referring to the weekends that I spent away from him.

I thought about it and talked it over with Rodney, who contested that his hope had always been to spend *more* time with me, not less. But when I told him that I wanted to save my marriage, that this was the only way, he eventually agreed.

Up until this time I had been seeing Rodney every other weekend.

We reduced this to once a month but made up for it by speaking more frequently on the phone, and when time and our schedules permitted we saw each other for a few short hours during the week.

It took months for John and me to rekindle what had become a fragile relationship, but twenty-five years on, we are still together and, although we have had a few long periods apart, I still have my relationship with Rodney.

KAREN'S STORY

Martin and I met at university and had been going out for five years before we got married. We were both in our early twenties and I remember my mother saying that we were too young to settle down and that we should live a little. But we were as certain as any young couple could be that we wanted to spend the rest of our lives together. The first year was wonderful; we were both working, earning good money and very much in love.

We hadn't planned to start a family so soon, but when Charlene came along a year later it didn't really matter because she was such a beautiful baby and Martin and I were both very happy.

I had intended to go back to work but after a few months and full of the joys of motherhood, I decided to stay at home with my baby. Looking back, this was probably the start of our problems. Suddenly, there was Charlene and me together twenty-four hours a day and then there was Martin working all hours to bring money into the house as we were missing my salary at the time.

This started to put a strain on our relationship and in the end I agreed to look for a part-time job and a childminder. The latter wasn't easy and after two false starts and with no immediate family around who could help me, I gave up.

Things were never the same after this, not even when Charlene started school and I was working again. But we struggled on. Then one evening, and quite out of the blue, Martin came in from work and said that he was leaving.

I was shocked at first and simply didn't know what to think or do. It was drastic, and unexpected. I tried to suggest that we arranged counselling or at least tried to do something, because it wasn't that our marriage was intolerable, we just didn't connect in the way we used to. But Martin had made up his mind and nothing I could say would change it.

After a few months I realised that if we had been honest with each other we would have owned up sooner to the fact that we had grown out of love, and that there simply wasn't enough to sustain the relationship. Not even our beautiful little girl.

Charlene was devastated and it was hard to cope with her tears and tantrums, especially when she asked why she couldn't have a father like all the other children. It took a long time for me to explain that her dad hadn't left her, he had left me, and that he would always be there for her. Martin, I must admit, continued to play his part and she was able to spend time with him. But things changed again when he moved away and wasn't able to see her as often. These were difficult times emotionally and financially, and although I didn't know it then, trying so desperately hard to be both mother and father meant that I was becoming less of myself.

Charlene became the centre of my world, and friends and family cautioned me about letting her have too much of her own way. I was also warned about the dangers of overcompensating – 'spare the rod and spoil the child' was a phrase whispered to me more than once. But I felt Charlene was my responsibility: we had, I thought, a wonderful relationship. She had been through enough and was deserving of everything I could give her.

Charlene was an intelligent and lively child and it took little encouragement for her to become involved in a whole range of after-school activities; I was only too happy to encourage her. The to-ing and fro-ing throughout the week, and swimming and dance sessions on Saturdays were tiring. But still, I was enjoying my role as the single parent raising an energetic and sociable child and giving her every opportunity to develop. It was fun and fulfilling getting to know my daughter and being able to appreciate her for the interesting, self-assured and challenging person that she was becoming.

We had developed a routine that worked for both of us – until Charlene decided on a further activity. She wanted to join the Brownies.

Now whilst I recognised the value of Brownies and all that it had to offer, Brownies night was on a Wednesday – the same night as my netball, the only activity I had kept for myself, a saving grace, a time to let off steam, be competitive, enjoy adult company and maintain my fitness. I managed to avoid saying no to Brownies, hoping Charlene would let it pass but just before her babysitter, Brenda, was due to arrive and I was half into my trainers, she started to complain that it was Wednesday and she wanted to go to Brownies.

I reminded her that Brenda came every Wednesday evening because it was the only evening that Mummy went out to play netball, and then I beckoned her to sit with me on the bed so that I could explain the routine we had that helped us both in what we wanted to do and what we had to do. I felt that she needed to understand that it was right and fair for both of us.

I could tell by her body language – tight-lipped and arms firmly folded around her – that Charlene would have none of it and she simply stormed out of the room when I had finished.

Tantrums continued the next morning and again after school. I thought that when reasoning failed, bribery had to be the next best thing, so I suggested that we picked up a takeaway and that later we could watch *The Little Mermaid*, our favourite video. In the end I was met with a nonchalant shrug of the shoulders and an unimpressed 'Whatever.' But nothing prepared me for the shock when she stroppily told me, just before going to bed, that 'Good mothers are supposed to make sacrifices for their children!'

I was astounded and left to wonder where this had come from. The television? Some book she had read? A cartoon character? Other children? I just didn't know. Then I started to feel guilty, thinking that I was still not doing enough and questioned just how the two hours a week I had given myself to play netball could possibly result in me being a 'bad mother'?

I felt so angry and upset with what Charlene had said that I slept very little that night. Her words had cut deeply and left me in turmoil, and there was no Martin to share the load.

I thought about the little clashes we had, like the day we were out shopping for clothes and she didn't like the ones I was choosing for her. We had reached a compromise when I suggested that she could choose for herself one of the dresses I was going to buy. But this situation was different.

Later I rebuked myself for softening up as Charlene's hurtful words once again played on my mind. No doubt, whenever I agreed to what she wanted, I was a 'good mother', but now that I wouldn't give in on the Brownie's issue, this evidently made me a bad one.

I knew my daughter was a determined person, but I had never seen her behave like this before. Was I to blame for her self-centred behaviour, for having given in too easily in the past? But this was the only way I knew of making up for what she had been through.

After a few more hours spent thinking it all through, I eventually decided that I would not give in to what I considered to be the manipulations of a child. At the age of seven, Charlene was old enough to understand that I too had a life and that my needs were just as important as hers.

The bottom line, selfish or not, was that I loved playing netball. I had excelled at it in school, played town and county and could even have made the national team. I was *not* going to give it up. And so, as the dawn chorus sounded, I resolved that if this was to be a battle of wills with that 'sweet' little girl of mine, I sure as hell was going to come out on top.

Invigorated and refreshed by my new-found confidence, I bravely brought up the subject over breakfast. Steadfast against the odd rolling of the eyeballs, shrugging of the shoulders and sudden interest in our cream-coloured ceiling, I described in detail the arrangement we had, feeling the need to convince Charlene that rather than being a 'bad mother' I was more of a deserving one, particularly in view of the 'numerous' sacrifices I had already made and from which she had benefited.

Knowing that Charlene was more than capable of understanding all that I had been saying, I decided to wait for her to respond and it was during this time that I realised that a preoccupation with my own feelings of guilt, of being under siege and having failed as a mother, was preventing me from considering how Charlene herself had been feeling. Only then did it occur to me that I should ask why going to Brownies was so important to her.

The response was instant.

'Because Donna goes and she says it's great. She says you can go on trips, play games, build things, go to the woods, make a lot of new friends and do things like arts and crafts which is what I like to do most.'

'But you can do most of that at school,' I argued.

'Yes, I know, Mum, but it's not like school. I can predict what is going to happen at school, but you don't always know what you are going to do at Brownies. Also, there aren't any teachers telling you what to do; you have helpers who have names like birds and they help you do what you want to do.'

'I see.' And I did. I had always encouraged Charlene to express her feelings and yet I had not been open to receive them. Most of what she did was routine, on her own, like her piano lessons, or with me. She was now telling me that she wanted to do something that was different, more stimulating and exciting. It was also clear that she wanted to experience this with her best friend, Donna, and not even mother love could compete with that. In the event, a possible solution thankfully presented itself.

It so happened that Donna lived less than a mile away and almost en route to netball, and so I called Mary, her mother, and told her of my dilemma.

There appeared to be some conspiracy between the girls. Donna had persisted about Brownies for weeks until her mother gave in, and no doubt was encouraging Charlene to do the same. It wasn't a problem for Mary because she and Steve, Donna's father, shared the 'dropping offs' and 'picking ups' of their three children. We laughed as Mary told me that with hindsight she wished she had left learning to drive until her children were old enough to drive themselves around the place.

It was then that I asked if she or Steve would be good enough to take Charlene to Brownies with Donna; in exchange, I could pick them both up afterwards. Mary was delighted to help and said nothing about the extra half-hour Charlene would have to spend with them before being taken to Brownies.

In breaking the news to Charlene I sat down with her and explained that I had found a way for her to go to Brownies without giving up my netball, and said that it would be her responsibility to organise herself and to be punctual.

She was overjoyed and ran to the phone to call Donna and to thank Mary for her kindness. Later, and in her own inimitable way, Charlene told me that she had not wanted me to give up my netball. She had just wanted to be able to go to Brownies. Of course she did, but I was too deep into my reactive martyrdom mode to have realised.

Needless to say, a lighter and more harmonious atmosphere returned to our household and I even found myself, on the Wednesday that followed, playing netball with more of a 'spring in my feet'. The previous week had been awful and I had found it difficult to concentrate as I fought with the guilt of having left Charlene at home feeling so disgruntled that she hadn't even bothered to wave goodbye. It was quite a relief knowing that we were both happy with how things had worked out.

I was also amazed at how much other people wanted to help, not just Mary and Steve, but also my netball coach and colleagues during the training sessions. I needed to leave fifteen minutes earlier than everyone else so that I could be on time to pick up the girls, and so when it was my turn to take up my position on court, I was able to play a little longer than other members of the team so that I could make up for the time I would lose.

It was after this that I began to really find myself again, and could see that it was better for both of us if I lived my life *with* my daughter, instead of trying to live it *for* her. We both gained a lot from what had happened. Me, a new-found independence, an even closer relationship with my daughter and now and again an extra night out with the girls, and Charlene, well, all that Brownies had to offer. In fact, one of my most treasured photographs is of her in her gold-coloured uniform, brown belt and beret, making her 'Brownie' promise and receiving one of her many badges.

Some people may believe that I would have been well within my rights to say, 'No,' from the beginning, but if I had done I would have closed out the options without even having considered what they might have been. If I had initially said, 'Yes,' to Charlene and misguidedly given up my netball in the process, I would most probably have been bitter and resentful, especially as our team won the netball league that year!

But even more heart-warming was what happened as I relayed the story to her years later.

She was a teenager and had listened intently, laughing and

embarrassed, no doubt at her wilfulness. As I ended the story, she denied being awkward, hugged and thanked me anyway and then planted a kiss on my cheeks. It was worth having found a way.

SUMMARY

Both these stories stress the need for personal assertiveness. We all find ourselves in situations where, for all sorts of reasons, we put the interests of others before ourselves. Social convention encourages us to do this. It makes us seem understanding and sympathetic people. On the other hand, if we put our own interests first we run the risk of being labelled selfish, self-centred and egoistic.

But it does not have to be like this. What appear to be conflicting situations with only stark alternatives can, through negotiation, lead to compromise to 'Win Win' outcomes.

Cristiana's story brings this out in sharp reality. She is torn in her affections for two men – John, to whom she is married, and Rodney, her long-term lover. For many readers, this arrangement may seem unkind and unnatural, a situation in which Cristiana is having her cake and eating it, too. But the fact of the case is that she truly loves both men.

It would be too harsh a judgement to say that she is weak-willed and indecisive. On a number of occasions, and against her inner inclinations, she tries to break off her relationship with Rodney. But she finds she can't. And so the outcome is continuous negotiating between consenting parties so that each gets some personal benefit. It is 'Win Win' but with heavy emotional costs. The downside of any 'Win Win' is that it goes hand in hand with 'Lose Lose.' There is always a price to pay.

Karen's story confirms the importance of this. She feels completely obligated to her daughter, always wishing to put her interests before her own. She is the ideal, dedicated mother we all admire. Unfortunately, as is so often the case, the child exploits to the full her mother's sense of obligation. Again and again, she 'guilt-trips' her. That is until Karen finally decides to pursue her own personal wishes.

At first, she feels riddled with guilt and torn with conflict. But again, like Cristiana, she arrives at a compromise 'Win Win' solution. Through negotiation with her daughter and other involved parties, she is able to pursue her own interests while at the same time meeting Charlene's wishes. As this story illustrates, to arrive at 'Win Win' solutions requires skilful negotiation with other people. It becomes a matter of managing complex personal relations. It is rarely a case of one-to-one to get to 'Win Win'!

SELF-HELP TIPS

• Always go for 'Win Win' instead of putting yourself or the other person first.

• Our own self-interests are just as important as those of others.

• Because of the 'guilt-trip' and of emotional blackmail, it is always easy to forget about ourselves.

• Negotiating with another person inevitably involves others. Manage these networks carefully.

- Life is not a rehearsal. If we don't seize the opportunity to do what we want to do today, it may never come again.

IN THE CORPORATION

Success in the modern corporation is all about negotiation. We have to negotiate for pay increases and promotion with our bosses. We have to negotiate deals with clients. And we have to negotiate with our colleagues to get things done.

We can have all the technical skills in the world, but these alone will not get us up the corporate ladder and into the boardroom. We also have to be able to negotiate, to get to 'Yes Yes' or 'Win Win' solutions. We have to compromise and respect the interests of others.

Corporate leadership is almost entirely based upon effective negotiation. Without negotiating the commitment of staff, colleagues and other team members, corporate goals will not be achieved – at any level within the organisation.

Negotiating skills cannot be gained through a university degree. They cannot be purchased off the shelf at the local bookstore. They come from life experiences. It is through negotiating 'Win Win' solutions in our personal lives that we gain the skills needed for team leadership and the keys for opening up the door of the corporate boardroom.

CHAPTER THREE

JAYSHREE AND DIANA **Managing Conflict**

Many people see conflict as a natural disagreement between individuals and groups because of differences in values, beliefs and traditions. But although we may pride ourselves on being sensitive and tolerant, we cannot always be relied upon to consider the feelings of other people at a time when we are caught up in our own.

A friend once told us about driving down a side street where cars were double-parked. An oncoming car started along the same road and it soon became clear that one of them would have to stop to let the other through. In the event, neither of them did and an impasse ensued as each waited for the other to reverse. Our friend felt that he had right of way because he had been on the road well before the other driver appeared, and was prepared to sit it out. Luckily, three other cars came up behind him, leaving the other driver with no alternative but to give way.

Our friend was unashamedly triumphant. And the other man? No doubt he was furious.

Conflict, which is a key word in our everyday lives and experiences, can emerge out of anything and at any time. If left to fester it can destroy friendships, build resentment and is often the primary cause of long and lingering family feuds.

Although mediators, arbitrators and counsellors are there to help us, depending on the circumstance, we may have no other choice but to deal with it ourselves.

JAYSHREE'S STORY

It's hard to remember if there has ever been a time when I have not been in conflict in one way or another.

I was thirteen years old when I arrived in England from India, with my parents, two brothers and a younger sister. I went to a special school to learn English for about six months before going into the mainstream school. I wasn't really ready for this because I still didn't have a good enough command of the language and found it hard to keep up with the other children.

For a good two years I was bullied at school because I didn't fit in with my classmates and found it difficult to adapt to my new and rather affluent surroundings. Back home I had been used to a very simple village life where there were no newspapers, radios or television and where we children had to make our own entertainment.

I was very quiet and thought that if I got on with my schoolwork and kept myself to myself, no one would bother me. But I found I was wrong when some girls wrote nasty graffiti on the toilet door and scribbled my name underneath it. The teacher knew immediately that it wasn't me, mainly because I was unlikely to have thought of doing such a thing and in any case, I didn't even understand what it was that had been written. I knew who had done it and when the teacher asked me I told her.

I soon learned what it meant to be honest when everyone called me 'grasser' and I got bullied even more.

It reached the stage where I dreaded going to school and one morning I cried and pleaded with my parents not to make me go. But my father, who was strict on education, said that I had to. I couldn't tell him that I was being bullied because he wouldn't understand. Furthermore, he said that even if I were to die in the school I would get an education because that was why we had come to England.

I was good at maths and the teacher would use my work as an example in class. Although I got the name 'teacher's pet', other pupils would sometimes ask me to help them with their homework. I did, and that's how things started to get better for me.

I left school with good grades and went on to sixth-form college, where again I found it difficult to fit in. I was lacking in self-confidence and as I couldn't join in with the general conversations around boys, music, fashion or television soap operas, I simply had nothing to talk about.

Then one day a really good-looking guy walked past a few of us girls who were standing in the corridor waiting for our lecturer to arrive. I turned to the girl next to me and said, ' Oh, he's nice.' She seemed shocked at first and then started to laugh. I laughed too and that seemed to break the ice. The other girls joined in and suddenly I no longer considered myself to be an outsider. I never looked back after that.

At college I became very interested in gender studies and was awakened to the many ways in which society discriminates against women. This got me thinking about what was happening in my own community – where, for example, boys have the freedom to do as they please and can have careers whilst girls, apart from school or college, are almost always housebound and expected only to become wives and mothers.

A passion about the rights of women began to stir in me, and after delving further into matters relating to gender and equality, I found myself evolving from a reticent individual into a rather rebellious feminist – something that was unheard-of in our Hindu community and definitely not what my parents expected of me.

All too soon I was being tested on my new-found beliefs when my parents called me into the living room of our semi-detached house and began talking about arranging a marriage for me. My cousins, who were seventeen and eighteen, were all happily married, and at nineteen I was next in line. They were looking for me to be married within a year and brought out a photograph of a fairly presentable guy who they said would be coming along with his parents to meet me.

Even though I knew this was going to happen to me sooner or later, it still came as a shock. But it was a greater shock to my parents when I told them that I didn't want to get married.

I remember the look of horror on my father's face and how enraged he was that I had even dared to consider such a thing. He told me not to forget who I was and the responsibility I had to my family. But I knew who I was, and although I had a responsibility to my family I also had one to myself.

My mother was heartbroken and begged me not to be stubborn and difficult. I sat with her and explained that I wasn't ready to get married yet; I wanted to do other things with my life like travel, meet different people and take in new experiences.

She couldn't understand where I was coming from and kept saying that I should put such foolish thoughts out of my head and accept and be happy with the plans she and my father were making for me. Whilst I had no doubt that they wanted the best for me, I couldn't go along with their plans because they were far from being what I wanted for myself.

My father did not speak to me again for days, and when he did it was only to say that he felt sure that I had been brainwashed by Western society and that I should feel ashamed about neglecting my tradition and my duties as a woman. I tried to explain that, rather than neglecting my traditions and so-called duties, I was prepared to challenge them. But he wouldn't listen and appeared to be more concerned about what the elders in our community would think about his unruly and disobedient daughter.

For weeks after this, the atmosphere in our house was awful. Although my brothers were not bothered by my defiance, and in any case were out most of the time, my sister, who was more traditional and thought that I was being disrespectful, wouldn't speak to me; apart from the odd acknowledgement that I was still alive, neither would my parents.

It was clearly a battle of wills, but I wasn't going to give in, and I spent long and lonely hours in my room hoping desperately for peace to return to our household.

During my self-imposed isolation, I was able to think more about my situation, how it was affecting my family and me, and what I could do about it.

It is very much part of our culture for women to be passive and to put other people first, and although I feared what might happen if I stepped out of line I was sure that I would find the strength to cope.

I could well understand the pressures my parents were under, having to live up to what was considered right and proper in our community, and I knew that my present behaviour reflected poorly on them.

I wasn't a bad person and my parents knew that, but I would be judged as such by the community, simply because I didn't want to get married. It was particularly difficult for my father, who as head of the household would be criticised for not exercising enough control over his family.

It was around this time that I got my exam results for university and as a concession asked my parents to put off the idea of an arranged marriage for me until I had finished my degree. I reminded my dad about his eagerness for us all to have a good education, and said that I would find it difficult to give any serious consideration to marriage whilst I was studying.

I could see the relief on his face when, at last, he had a plausible reason that he could use for me not wanting to get married. It was a reason he knew would be readily accepted by the community because of their admiration for well-educated young people.

Making the most of this reprieve, I threw myself into my studies and was also able to focus on political and social policies. I joined a women's group and this further stimulated my interest in international development and the plight of women working in poor conditions or living in poverty in developing countries.

Having thought of nothing else for a few months, I made a firm decision to look for a job with the United Nations or to become a voluntary worker abroad once I had finished my degree. This was my long-term aim, and although I knew that I would be disappointing my parents, who were still looking to arrange my marriage, I had to let them know.

Rather than telling them outright, and provoking further arguments, I decided to introduce what I intended to do gradually. I took every opportunity to tell my family about my course and how it had got me thinking about my future and the kind of work I wanted to do. But although he listened my father wasn't at all impressed, and my heart sank as he told me that my future husband would probably not approve of my plans, especially when I could expect to have children soon after my marriage.

Although I was angry at what my father was saying, I decided that it was best not to react.

But there were times when I felt burdened by my circumstances and tried not to think about the hurt I was causing my parents. They were embedded in a society of customs that had directed their lives from birth and conditioned them to live in a certain way. But it was not like that for me. I had the means to create a different way of life for myself and that was exactly what I was going to do.

During the last eighteen months of my degree, my father, having chosen not to heed the notice of my ambitions, would now and again present me with photographs of young men, saying that he thought I should at least begin to plan ahead for my marriage. But I refused to meet any of them.

My mother, who had left it up to my father to bring me round to the idea of marriage, joined in by suggesting that I could even choose my husband, as long as he was from the same caste.

I did at one time think that my attitude to marriage would change, especially when I was attracted to a couple of guys at university. But it hadn't, and so my mother's suggestion, although it was a fair compromise, did not appeal to me.

Although I never really expected my parents to relent, it was wonderful when we were on good enough terms to enjoy family meals and celebrations or for me to go shopping with my mother.

But I was never really off my guard, particularly when I knew that my father was always looking for an excuse to bring up an argument around me. It would often stem from him feeling angry about something like my brother not turning up on time, if there was a problem with the car or even if someone had let him down at work. He would start by saying that his life was made miserable because of me, and he talked at length about the responsibility he had for a daughter who should have been married by now.

It was after one of these outbursts that I began to accept that my efforts to get through to my parents had failed. There was simply nothing else I could do to convince them that I wanted a different life from the one they were prescribing for me. But it wasn't just my parents I had to deal with.

My brothers, who were not under the same pressures, were quite civil. On the other hand, my younger sister would go for months without speaking to me because she was more into our culture, was concerned about family pride and wanted to get married. It was customary for the elder daughter – in this case me – to get married first, and she did not like having to wait.

Throughout my troubles, I was lucky to have a friend, Taj, to whom I could talk. She had had similar experiences but eventually gave in to family pressures and accepted an arranged marriage. Although her husband was more amenable than others and didn't mind her continuing with her career after they got married, she had to give up work when they decided to have children.

She explained that, although she felt that she had lost a little of herself, her life had become so much easier once she had agreed to an arranged marriage. She was very supportive and encouraged me to do whatever I thought was best for me.

I finished my degree and, with no further excuses, the pressure to get married gathered pace.

It was when I began to feel as if a heavy grey cloud was hanging over my family, one that was likely to send my father to an early grave, that I seriously considered giving in as Taj had done, or leaving home knowing that it would mean cutting all ties with my family and my community.

It wasn't easy, but, having done all I could to make my parents understand my point of view, and feeling sure I was doing the right thing for my family as well as myself, I decided to leave home.

My parents were devastated but, although it was going to be difficult on both sides, at least we could all move on in our lives.

DIANA'S STORY

I knew it was going to be hard when I left my husband Gary, but I also knew it was the only way that I could hang on to my sanity – and possibly even my life.

For years Gary had been verbally and physically abusive, and whilst I was strong enough to stand up to him, it was when my home was no longer a safe place to be in that I decided to leave and to file for divorce.

When I told Gary what I was going to do he didn't believe me, because I had threatened to leave once before, then had relented after his apologies and promise to end the abuse. But when, after two months of relative calm he started again, I realised that he was, in fact, never going to change and that it was in my best interest to leave him.

I should have guessed how difficult things were going to be when Gary started to turn our children, Miranda, who was five, and David, who was three, against me. He kept them close to him all the time, told them that I didn't love them and that I was doing everything I could to break up the family.

Knowing that once the divorce proceedings started I would have to continue living with him under the same roof, or risk losing the children if I left, I tried not to make the situation any worse by arguing with him, and simply continued to love and look after my children as I had always done.

Seeing that I was able to hold myself together, Gary switched from physical to emotional abuse. He would steal some of my clothes, shoes, jewellery and other personal items, wait for me to replace them, and then steal them again. When I asked what he had done with them, he would vehemently deny having taken anything that belonged to me and say that it was all in my mind.

He would sometimes race to pick up the children from our child minder when he knew I was on my way to get them. He did this not only to make me look foolish, but also for me to question my memory about the arrangements we had made around the children.

But worst of all was when he would sneak up behind me when I was doing things around the house like loading the washing-machine or cleaning the bathroom, or stand silently over me at times when I sat watching television or reading once the children had gone to bed.

His plan was clearly to force me out of the house so that he would be in a better position to get custody of the children. After six months, he succeeded. I simply could not continue to live with the relentless intimidation and the mental cruelty I was experiencing, and it was clear that the children were aware of the strained atmosphere in the house. I moved out and went back to my parents.

Gary applied for full custody of the children but the judge would not allow it and ruled instead for a fifty-fifty split when I said I would not oppose joint custody. Of course, I lost the house, but having reached a reasonable settlement I had enough money for a small deposit on another little house for my children and myself, and I hoped to be able to live my life there in peace and without fear.

When everything was finally settled after the divorce I didn't seek any form of maintenance from Gary because I didn't want any financial ties with him. We simply agreed that I would cover Miranda's needs and that he would cover David's.

Although a few people, including my parents, argued that I should have gone for full custody of the children, I felt the judge's decision was the right one. Anything else would have been unfair to the children, who were already experiencing the trauma of seeing their parents separate. Furthermore, I didn't want them in ten or fifteen years' time to blame me for them not having a relationship with their father or for him to do the same.

Although Gary had never been violent towards the children, he failed to see how his actions were affecting them, and whilst I endeavoured to ensure that the children maintained a loving relationship with him, he seemed incapable of doing the same for me.

On Father's Day, at Christmas or on his birthday, I would go with the children to choose a present or card for him, and had every intention of doing so until they reached the age when they could make decisions for themselves.

Yet on Miranda's birthday, which fell on one of the days when it was his turn to have the children, Gary changed his telephone number so that I couldn't call her up and wish her a Happy Birthday. I knew full well that he would have told her that I didn't care, and that here was the proof.

Even though I was upset, I didn't raise it with her or with him because I didn't want to get into a situation where the children had to think about which one of us was lying to them.

This might all seem very noble of me, but there were times when I wished that I could put my children and myself on a plane, fly away and never come back, or when I longed to do some damage to this man, to pay him back for what he was putting me through. But I couldn't because of the children – and in any case, to harm him as I was sorely tempted to do would have made me as bad as him.

A few months ago I had an opportunity to take the children abroad on holiday, but Gary would not give me their passports. Yet he could take them out of the country at any time – and has threatened to do so. It is a constant worry for me whenever the children are with him because there is always a feeling that I might not see them again.

It once got to the stage where I was so beside myself that I went to seek legal advice, thinking that it would help to allay my fears, but when I was told that I first had to *prove* that my husband was going to abduct the children, I was left feeling worse than ever. There was nothing I could do to prove it.

It was obvious that Gary was trying to make my life a misery, and the more I withstood the pressure, the harder he tried. If I had ended up on the street, or had remained at my mother's house, living from hand to mouth, he would been happy because it would show, as he had often said, that I couldn't survive without him. But I knew that he was troubled by the fact that I was not only surviving but also doing a lot better for myself.

Except over the children I didn't need to see or speak to Gary. But if something was wrong with either of them when it was his turn to have them, I would phone to explain, so that if they needed medical attention he would have some history about the problem. But he wouldn't do the same for me and I couldn't force him to communicate in that way.

The trauma of our divorce affected the children, and it was a very sad day when I had to register Miranda with a child psychologist. She was nine years old and talking about killing herself. Gary couldn't see that his behaviour was directly affecting her, and because she talked about it with me he surmised that I was the one who was causing the problem. It simply didn't occur to him that she wasn't comfortable talking to him about her feelings.

Miranda didn't like his new partner, nor the fact that her bedroom was being used as a dumping ground, and she couldn't understand why Gary often left her alone inside the house whilst he was outside playing football with her brother.

The effect on David was different. Whereas Miranda was more inclined to keep things to herself, David had become very abusive and violent, and I was increasingly being called to the school because he was swearing and hitting out at other children.

David was close to his father, and if ever I had to reprimand him he would throw a tantrum and say that he wanted to go to his dad. At these times, I would not hesitate to pick up the phone and let him speak to his father and arrange for him to go over. It was up to Gary to tell David whether or not he could have him, because I wanted my son to know that I would not stop him being with his father if he really wanted to be.

The turmoil was relentless and, although my friends and family were amazed at how strong I was being, I was really only able to cope at times by finding a release that didn't aggravate the pain, like having a glass of wine. It helped me to relax and lose the edge of my anger.

But even so, when the pressure became too great to be relieved by alcohol, I would feel myself falling into a deep depression, which could last anything between a few hours and a whole day.

At such times, everything felt dark and dismal. I cried as loudly as I needed to when I was on my own, but when the children were with me I did so quietly. But I was never ashamed to let them see me cry because I didn't want them to think that there was anything wrong with crying, or that I didn't have feelings and could cope with everything.

In many ways, the break-up of my marriage has taught me how to manage my emotions. It was hard at first to get to grips with myself, especially when I was angry or felt like shouting at the children. This was until I realised that I didn't just want to shout at them for something they had done, but *also* for what someone else might have done, whether it was their father, or a colleague at work. It was important for me to accept that there was always a danger that I could take out on them the frustration that had been building up inside me.

It could not have been easy for the children, having to live in two separate houses, and it was therefore my responsibility to make sure that their lives were as comfortable and as straightforward as possible, without spoiling them.

They saw Gary's place as home because it was where we had all been living together, but where I lived was referred to as *Mummy's house*. I enjoyed making it into a home for them so that they really liked coming over to stay. I tried to do this in many ways, like decorating their rooms in colours they had chosen. But I also made sure that when they came back from their father's house, I asked a little about what they had been doing. I was not interested in Gary's life, but I didn't want the children to think that once they crossed the doorstep to Mummy's house part of their life must end until the next time they saw their father.

It is still hard going at times, especially when I am unsure about what Gary is likely to do next. One of the last things he said when I finally left him was that he was going to kill me and the children, and then he would commit suicide.

But I came to the conclusion that if I continued to listen to his threats I would be too afraid even to step outside my front door, and I didn't want that. What I want is to love my children and to be able to live my life as a mother and as an individual.

SUMMARY

Jayshree's story is of a very common experience for someone torn between two cultures. She is faced with conflicting pressures from the wishes of her parents and her own personal ambitions.

In this situation there is little chance of arriving at a 'Win Win' outcome. Her parents have a fixed view that she should get married as soon as possible and to a man of her father's choosing. Her mother has little say in this and has to go along with her husband's wishes. Her sister's desire to get married also adds to the pressures.

Studying for a degree does not solve Jayshree's problems. Her academic studies allow her to retreat into denial, but this can only be a temporary solution. Ultimately she will have to face up to her situation and make a life-changing decision.

This decision will have consequences not only for herself but for a broader network of family and friends. The outcome for herself will be ostracism and loneliness, family rejection and the casting aside of an emotional support system. This is the price she is prepared to pay to do what she wants to do.

But is she being selfish? Her parents, younger sister and other family members probably think she is. But where do we draw the line between selfishness and personal assertiveness? Do others have the right to dictate to us how we should live our lives? In this case, isn't it the parents, particularly the father, who are being selfish? Sometimes, it is impossible for us to manage cultural diversity. We are forced into tough decisions, which take us in one direction rather than another.

Diana's story is another account of a relationship that goes wrong because of the selfishness and emotional problems of a male partner. Instead of the break-up of the relationship being handled in a mature manner, her partner creates conflicts. The children are the focal point for this and they become nothing more than pawns in an ongoing row between their parents. They are the bargaining tools, or the resources, that are exploited to act out the drama between two adults. Again, there appears to be little chance of both parties getting to 'yes' in a compromised 'Win Win' situation. It is a battle of strengths with the children stuck in the middle.

SELF-HELP TIPS

• Taking into account the complexity of the human condition, sometimes 'Win Win' is not an option. Instead, we have to set our goal and go for it.

- Our wants and preferences are as important as those of others. Why should we allow theirs to dominate our own?

- Conflicts rarely have immediate solutions. Strategies have to be carefully thought through.

- Give yourself time to think. Weigh up the alternatives and consider the possible outcomes of different decision-making routes.

IN THE CORPORATION

Corporations are full of conflicts. They are made up of people running their own personal agendas. There are colleagues with inflated egos, who are entirely selfish and who show absolutely no consideration or understanding of the interests of others.

But there are also conflicts surrounding a broad range of moral issues. Decisions have to be taken that can affect the quality of people's lives and their relationships with others. There are also other conflicts that arise when companies force their employees to participate in what they consider to be unethical practices.

This means that we are often forced into making difficult decisions. There can be no opportunity for negotiation or compromise, and we have to choose one direction rather than another.

To be successful in the modern corporation, it is necessary to be decisive, to manage conflicts through self-confident decision-making – and to live with the consequences. Those who get into the corporate boardroom display these very characteristics. They are prepared to stand up and be counted on the basis of their actions.

CHAPTER FOUR

CONNIE AND MADELINE **Handling Crises**

Life is looking good. The kids are doing well at school, the bills are no longer a headache, you are enjoying your job, you have trusted friends and your relationship is thriving. Then, without warning, misfortune strikes and before long you find yourself in the middle of a crisis much worse than you could have possibly imagined.

Everything around you begins to fall apart and you are left to wonder how and why this is happening. It is not of your making but you are expected to repair the damage, counter the shame and, most importantly, protect your children.

With your emotions in turmoil, just where do you start and what exactly do you do?

Rebuke yourself for a lack of foresight and failure to heed the warnings? Call upon the social network that women are so good at creating? Look to your family for support, or decide that you are strong enough to manage it alone?

Whatever your decision, it is important to prepare for the challenges ahead, knowing that you will have to face disappointments and setbacks. You may even have to face crises which require every ounce of your strength and determination.

But it is possible that from these life-changing experiences there will emerge an even stronger you.

CONNIE'S STORY

I really should have listened to all those people who had warned me about Dexter, but they say that love is blind and in my case it definitely was.

Before I met Dexter I had been doing pretty well for myself, moving from being a cash-strapped single parent to a highly sought-after fashion designer. People were full of praise for me, but only I knew how hard it had been to make something of myself.

One of four children, I was a bit of an outcast and not such a 'pretty one' as some of my relatives used to say. School was an absolute nightmare for me because I wasn't very good at writing and could hardly read. Even so, teachers who knew the problems I had still called me up in front of the class to read so that other children could laugh at me. I was the class idiot and was bullied for years until I decided I wasn't going to take any more.

Although being able to stand up for myself gave me a lot of self-confidence it didn't help my education because I still couldn't read or write properly and so left school without any qualifications.

But I knew how to survive and that's what I was doing when I found myself at nineteen years old living in a high-rise flat with two children and no money. For about four years I had to literally beg, steal and borrow from family and friends.

I started making clothes for my children and myself because I couldn't afford to buy them, and then began sewing for friends who would pay me. Encouraged by a few people who saw and liked my designs, I decided to set up a business. I got advice and support from our local enterprise agency and went into partnership with two friends.

After eighteen months and a lot of hard work, contracts were rolling in, as were bookings for fashion shows and requests for television and news coverage and magazine articles. There was also a stream of beautiful young women and dazzling young men, all wanting to model our designs.

But nothing lasts for ever and after four years at the top things started to turn sour. The two girls I was in partnership with moved on to other things, and although I chose to stay with the business I couldn't really manage on my own. Then I met Dexter.

He was a steward at the place where I held one of my last fashion shows and had offered to help me pack and load my stuff on to the van. Dexter was literally a romantic hero – tall, dark and handsome – and I was very much attracted to him. We started to go out together.

After years of hard slog and no time for a serious relationship, it was good to be close to someone again. Dexter was easy to talk to, and when I told him that I no longer felt able to run the business on my own, he offered to help out, but his suggestion that we set up our own mobile fast-food business was far more attractive as we would be working together and, once we had a licence, there would be a quick turnover with little outlay. I closed my business and re-invested in our new partnership.

Selling drinks, burgers, kebabs, chips, pasties and hot-dogs outside concert halls, clubs, festivals and local music events was a poor substitute for the glitz of the fashion industry, but being with the man I loved made up for that, and we were making money.

I can't quite remember when it all started going wrong and I guess I could have been in denial.

Dexter would go missing for days at first and then it became weeks. I had no idea where he was going or what he was doing, and he became aggressive when I asked. Then he started knocking me around for no reason and I sometimes ended up staying indoors waiting for the bruises to heal.

After eighteen months of this I was unable to cope, physically or mentally, so we had to close the business.

This was the perfect time for me to get out of the relationship, but I didn't and we continued to see each other on and off for another three years.

Dexter lived on the ground floor of a block of flats. One afternoon when I was visiting him during a more harmonious period of our relationship, we heard loud banging and I remember screaming at Dexter, 'Someone is trying to break down the door! Call the police!' Imagine my confusion when I looked out of the window and saw that it *was* the police who had surrounded the flats with four cars and one van and were trying to force themselves in.

It all happened so quickly. I remember standing in the corner of the room, shaking with fear as I watched four policemen get hold of Dexter and march him out of the door. Then another two of them came over to me, asked if I was Connie Sinclair and, when I nodded, said that they were arresting me for drug trafficking.

They took me back to my house and started turning the place upside down.

After searching the house for an hour, interrogating me as they went from room to room, they took my computer, a few boxes and some papers. They then handcuffed me and bundled me into a back of the police car. I still couldn't believe what was happening to me – why I was being treated like a criminal when I had done nothing wrong.

My two girls, April and Candice, who were by then in their early teens, had gone to friends after school and I was thankful for that, because it would have upset them terribly to see how I was being treated.

At the police station I was put into a small room while I waited for the duty solicitor to arrive. I had four interviews and was constantly being asked about the people that Dexter had been associating with. I couldn't give the police any answers. I was more than a little suspicious about the expensive jewellery he often wore, but he told me they were gifts from some of his women friends. I did suspect that he might have been involved in other things but I never dared to ask. The police didn't believe me and continued with some very harsh questions.

When I realised that they were going to keep me in the cell overnight, I told them that I was concerned about my children and was allowed to phone my elder sister, Monica. She had never liked Dexter and was always on at me to finish the relationship. In the end, and just to keep her off my back, I lied and told her that I had. Now she had found out the truth in the worst possible way. I listened to her screaming at me down the phone and then tried to reassure her that I had done nothing wrong.

As I didn't want the girls to learn about what had happened over the phone, in case they needed support I asked Monica to go to my house and speak with them direct and then to take them home with her.

Having to sleep in the cell was an absolute nightmare. There was only a wooden bench with a thin mattress, the toilet was just a little metal bowl in the corner and I had no privacy whatsoever.

In the morning, after my sister had arranged bail for me, I took a cab to her house. April and Candice had gone to school, which helped because it gave me time to gather myself and to have a much-needed bath.

As I sank into the bubbles, I began to realise the severity of what I was being charged with. My biggest fear was having to tell my parents, but I knew that if I didn't the press certainly would – and they did.

Local radio stations, television and newspapers carried the story, and I sat numbly in the corner as my sister read out the banner headlines, '*Local woman held for drug trafficking and money laundering*'. I had warned my parents, but even so did not expect anything like the publicity that was generated.

I had always hoped for my moment of fame on the television, but had never dreamed that it would be like this. Deep down I knew that I should have left Dexter long ago, when I had the chance, and this thought played over and over in my mind.

When all is said and done, it wasn't the crime that made me feel ashamed and guilty, because I was not involved in pushing drugs. It was the lies I had told people who were concerned about me, pretending that I had finished my relationship with Dexter. The fact that they would now all find out that I had lied was my biggest shame. I had deceived the very people I was now looking to for support.

The first few days after my arrest were the worst in my life. I didn't want to wake up, and wished that I could have died in my sleep. But my girls helped me to survive. Whilst I was being judged out there by people who didn't even know me, they were more concerned about who was going to make me breakfast or go shopping with me as I couldn't face going out on my own. If they were having a hard time at school, which I suspect they were, they simply didn't show it.

Still worse was yet to come when, during a mix-up in the court hearing, I had to spend a night in a women's prison and travelled there in a 'meat wagon' with other prisoners.

It was a stroke of luck that in the same van was an old friend of mine, Rachel. She knew the ropes because she was often in and out of prison, and said she would help me to get extra pants, tea bags, sugar and biscuits from the stores the women had organised for themselves. I was so grateful.

I didn't sleep a wink all night, thinking about what was happening to me. Then, all of a sudden, I realised that this situation could not last for ever. When it was over, I promised myself that I would get my life back under control.

What I wanted most, of course, was to be set free, but I had to consider the alternative: being sent to jail. The more I thought about the case – transactions I had made to Dexter's personal account when it was being monitored by Customs and Excise, and the Mercedes we had bought in my name, and the expensive holidays we had taken – the harder I felt it was going to be to prove my innocence.

In view of this I began to make plans for my children, who would look after them and how I would prepare them for the possibility of their mother going to jail. There were other things I would have to sort out like finances, the house, the car and other personal belongings. Focusing my thoughts in this way brought a kind of relief I hadn't felt for weeks.

By morning I was beginning to feel better about myself, because I had acknowledged the mountain I had to climb and had started to gather the strength I was going to need to help me reach the top.

At breakfast I sat with Rachel, who introduced me to some of her mates. They were all very friendly and promised to help make me feel at home.

Lisa, who was in for doing drugs and was 'top dog' of the section I was in, invited me up to her cell. She wanted to know more about my case and, after I told her, took me through the court proceedings, told me what to expect and how I was to prepare myself. She then said her next best advice was for me to take a few pills because it would help me deal with life inside. As phone-cards were a luxury, I would have no problem exchanging them for drugs. I was grateful for the advice, but even if 'pills' were a sure way of coping with the harshness of prison life, I was determined not to take them.

Later that morning I was taken back to court and I was released on bail in the afternoon.

It seems crazy, but that short spell in prison really helped me to focus my thoughts. Although it was the last place I would have chosen to reflect in, I needed space away from the turmoil around me. It made me decide that I would no longer hide away and be fearful of what might happen. I would instead prepare myself to manage, come what may.

I had been running a small boutique when the case broke and had reached a mutual agreement with the owner, not to return. I knew the case would probably take some time to get to court, and in the meantime I needed a job to tide me over.

It was hard going and at times it seemed like the whole town was against me; friends who I had hoped would support me were no longer there, and I was constantly being turned down for jobs I was more than capable of doing.

Eventually I found a vacancy in a restaurant. After I had told my boss about my situation, he said I could stay but that I had to work in the kitchen. And so I did; I washed up, swept up, polished up and mopped up, because if nothing else I was going to make sure that we had the cleanest kitchen in town! There was no time for self-pity. I had been given a chance and I was going to make the most of it.

During the year that followed I went to court nine times before my solicitor informed me that all charges were being dropped. However, it wasn't until I actually received the acquittal in writing that I believed that it was all over.

The girls were ecstatic and my parents relieved. There were many tears and it was at that time I realised how lucky I was to have such a supportive family.

At last I was free, not only from the charges that had almost destroyed my life but also from Dexter, who was found guilty and received a lengthy jail sentence. He had been the middleman negotiating the deals but had not handled the drugs himself.

Amongst many other things, the experience taught me how important it is to face, head on, whatever it is that is going on in your life and to find ways of dealing with it. At last, I am the one in control of my life.

MADELINE'S STORY

When I look back at my life it appears that I have simply been going from one crisis to another. But nothing could have prepared me for the pain and anguish of the last few years.

I was brought up in a very strict Christian family, and although my parents approved of me having a boyfriend when I was sixteen, they didn't expect me to get pregnant. But I did and was forced to marry my baby's father, Byron, so as not to bring shame onto the family.

It was a mistake, and only the birth of our first child, Sabrina, six months later, brought any kind of reprieve in our relationship. Even so, we had another two children, David and Tricia, and stayed together for almost fifteen years until I told Byron to leave when I could no longer put up with his abusive behaviour and string of affairs.

The children were devastated because, although their father and I had our differences, it was never in front of them and they couldn't really understand why he was leaving.

I was taking a university degree in Humanities at the time and working part-time to supplement the family income, and whilst I knew that things were going to be difficult when Byron left, I didn't expect to be served with an eviction order and given seven days to leave our home.

We were thousands of pounds in arrears on the house because we had taken out a second mortgage for home improvements and Byron had decided months before he left that he wasn't going to pay a penny towards what we owed or for the children.

I went to see a debt settlement agency which I thought would help, but was told that I had left it all too late and there was nothing they could do. I couldn't accept this, and, after deciding there was no way I could allow my children and me to be put out on the streets, I made an appointment to see our bank manager.

After I told him what had happened and showed him that I had an income through my work, and could increase my hours to get more if I needed to, he said they were prepared to rescind the eviction order and reduce the payments. But this was dependent on me getting a divorce so that my husband's name could be removed from the deeds and I was sole owner.

Byron did not contest the divorce, and after a few years of hard work and some creative budgeting I managed to pay off the arrears and make a small profit from the sale of the house. I then rented a property from our local housing association.

The next few years were wonderful. Even though the house was much smaller than the one we had had before, we made it into a happy home, and having to be both mother and father to my children brought them closer to me.

By that time I had passed my degree, had a full-time job as a lecturer, and was very active in my local church and the community. The children saw very little of their father in the years that followed, and although he briefly showed up at Sabrina's wedding it was as if he had never really featured in their lives.

When the children became adults, they urged me to make a life for myself, and Tricia, who was the last to leave home when she decided to live with her boyfriend, Peter, made me promise that I would. During the years that I had spent being there for all three of my children, I had never really had time to think about a life of my own, and before I even had a chance to, three grandchildren had already arrived and I was helping to look after them.

I was proud of my family, and was delighted when Tricia announced that she was pregnant. Unlike her sister and brother, Tricia saw no point in getting married, and this caused the break-up of her relationship with Peter. They had been living together for three years, and seven months into her pregnancy she left him and moved back into the house with me.

In spite of the circumstances, it was wonderful having my daughter and my beautiful grandson, Daniel, living with me. I felt that there was a special bond between Daniel and myself because I was there when he was born and held him even before his mother was able to because of the difficult time she had giving birth.

Daniel was a happy child, with gorgeous brown eyes and a smile that could melt your heart. I was glad to have been playing such a big part in his life when he was a baby and this continued even after his mother had moved to her own place. She would take him to school in the mornings and I would pick him up in the afternoons, then he would stay with me until she came home from work.

One Saturday morning as Daniel was playing in the garden a few weeks after his fourth birthday, I noticed that he had small reddish spots on his arms. Knowing that there was a spate of chicken pox going around in the school, we saw little cause for concern, especially as he appeared to be his usual boisterous self. On Sunday the change in him was not dramatic but noticeable as he appeared lethargic and was lying around more on the settee.

On Monday morning as I was getting ready for work, Tricia called to say that Daniel had been vomiting and after taking him to the doctor she was told that if he did not improve by Tuesday, she was to call again. She had to, because by then the spots were spreading and he continued to vomit. The doctor diagnosed chicken pox and prescribed some tablets and a lotion.

I called in to see Daniel after work and was immediately distressed by what I saw. The spots were not only covering the whole of his body, but looked inflamed and were weeping. But even more worrying was that his little hands had started to turn purple. I immediately dialled 999, and within minutes of me explaining Daniel's condition two ambulances arrived outside Tricia's house.

I got into one of the ambulances with Daniel and his mother and as we sped along the road, sirens blasting, I tried to keep his spirits up by saying that when he was better he would be able to boast to his friends about having travelled in an ambulance. On any other occasion, knowing Daniel, it would have been exciting for him to think that he was experiencing something none of his friends had. But he hardly responded and it was then that I realised that something was seriously wrong with my grandson.

After receiving the results of blood samples the doctor had taken soon after we arrived at the hospital, we were told it was possible that Daniel had contracted a contagious disease. Confounded by the news, we had to wait another two hours before they announced that he would have to be moved to a specialist hospital and another three before being told that there were no beds at the specialist hospital. Alarmingly, another two hours elapsed before a place was eventually found for Daniel at a local hospital for children.

Once we arrived at the hospital for children, we expected that the medical staff would tend to Daniel, but apart from taking from us the medication the doctor had prescribed for him, and putting him in a side cubicle, they did nothing else. By now Daniel was lying quite still and I was worried about the slight swelling on the left side of his face. He couldn't eat and wouldn't drink, and even though I asked the hospital staff about giving him a drip, I was simply told that the needle would upset him and that there was no need for a drip.

My daughter, who was more trusting of the staff than I was, said he was in the right place, and she was sure that he would be looked after. But I was beside myself because, although I kept asking the hospital staff to treat Daniel, they did nothing, and I began to wonder whether, even without any medical training, I was the only one who could see that his condition was getting worse.

My daughter, who had stayed with him overnight, decided to go home to change whilst I kept vigil by his side. I held his hand and whilst he looked hot and was shaking, his skin was cold and clammy. But it was when I noticed that his tongue was bleeding that I panicked and called the doctor. For the first time in almost twenty-four hours, they started to treat him by spraying some white liquid on his tongue. Whatever it was, it must have been potent, because it made him jump and his eyes, which up until that time had been closed, opened with terror. They left the bottle with me, saying that I could use it if his tongue started bleeding again.

When Tricia returned, I told her what had happened. Not someone who would normally panic, she simply pulled her chair close to his bedside, and began speaking to him softly, in the hope that he would respond. But he didn't and I began praying to God that I was wrong in thinking that he was slipping away.

Deep down in my heart I wanted to stay with my grandson but, for the first time since his mother and I had been sharing his upbringing, it felt like I was encroaching. It was as if something was telling me that at this time it was right for Tricia to be alone with her son. And so, with a very heavy and lonely heart, I left the two of them at eleven o'clock that evening.

At nine o'clock the next morning, the phone rang and a voice said, 'Mrs Granger, could you please get down to the hospital as soon as you can.' I tried to, but by the time I got there, my dear little grandson was dead.

My daughter had been rocking and singing to him when his body went limp in her arms. When I got to the ward, I couldn't recognise Daniel. His face was disfigured by the swelling which had started when he first arrived at the hospital, and it was as though he had been battered and bruised. My daughter collapsed in my arms and wept. I was distraught, and along with a whole range of pain and emotions that welled up inside of me was the question 'Why?'

There were no answers, and staff at the hospital said they were stunned at what had happened, and that Daniel had died from what they thought was 'streptococcal septicaemia'. The post mortem later revealed that it was a rare case of meningitis. The bacteria had poisoned his blood and by the time he died there was only one-third of fluid left in his body.

My daughter was devastated, and as we travelled home without our dearest little boy there were no words I could find that would comfort her. It was then I decided that someone had to answer for what had happened to Daniel.

Sabrina and David were there to console their sister as I started legal proceedings. I was bitter and angry, and wanting the world to know how much we had suffered, I called the press and told them that the hospital had murdered my grandson. They covered the story with interviews and photographs, and people who did not even know that Daniel had been taken ill were stopping us in the streets, crying and giving their condolences. Many of Daniel's friends brought flowers, cards and little teddy bears, and his school closed for the day out of respect for him. Nobody could believe what had happened.

I found a lawyer who took up the case and we started by fighting for a judicial review, which we hoped would lead to there being an inquest. We didn't get it, and four weeks later Daniel's body was released for burial. People lined the streets as the funeral cortège passed, and although it was wonderful to see the amount of support we had it was the darkest and saddest day of my life.

But the legal battle continued, with me at the forefront, fighting for the hospital to admit to negligence. Throughout the many letters and the caseloads that went to and fro, and the legal appearances and delaying tactics that were being deployed, I never once wavered, or felt like giving up. I was determined to keep strong for my daughter so that she was left to grieve for her needless and most tragic loss.

Our life was never going to be the same without Daniel, and weeks after his death I was still going to school to pick him up, even though I knew that he would not be there.

It was three years before we finally won the case, when the hospital admitted negligence.

A letter arrived around Christmas-time and in a strange kind of way, although we knew the hospital was in the wrong, we were still hoping that they would have come up with some kind of excuse, like Daniel having had a heart defect that no one knew about, because knowing that they could have saved him made the loss even more difficult to bear.

We also learned from the letter that if Daniel had been allowed to take the tablets he had been prescribed by his GP, the ones the hospital staff had taken away from him, it was possible that he might have survived.

It was only after the case was over that I felt able to grieve for Daniel, and had to have some bereavement counselling to help me through the process.

Daniel's life was short, but I would have given anything to have relieved the agony and pain that he suffered in his last hours.

Summary

Everything seems to be going well. Then suddenly, out of the blue, our lives are turned upside down. This is what happens to Connie and Madeline. Both are unprepared for what is about to hit them. But in handling these emergencies, they manage to work out strategies that let them get on with their lives and do what they feel needs to be done.

Connie is the naive one. She has been living in a violent relationship

– and how can she not have known where her boyfriend's money was coming from? A woman driven by emotion and passion, it is only when she is arrested by the police that she is compelled to face up to herself and assess her situation. The trauma of this arrest forces her to work out coping strategies for her children. This requires her to swallow her pride and to exploit the goodwill of her sister.

Her spell in prison highlights to her the fact that she will have difficulty in getting a job afterwards, but she desperately needs one in order to be allowed to look after her children and to carve out an independent life for herself. These pressures give her the determination to make a go of it. She does this by taking any job and making a success of it, but her greatest prize is the self-respect she regains when finally the charges against her for fraud and drug-trafficking are dropped.

If Connie is the victim of her own self-imposed problems, this is not the case for Madeline, who shows, well before the tragic loss of her grandson, that she can deal with crises. In debt, threatened with losing her home, and with three children to support, she does not panic. Instead, she goes to her bank manager and negotiates a solution.

Few words can express the sorrow felt at the death of a child, and there is not much that can be done other than to develop coping strategies. In these, Madeline not only relies heavily on family and friends but also the public at large to help her come to terms with the loss of her grandson.

All crises have legacies which can either create problems for the future or help the aggrieved to recover. In Madeline's case by taking legal action against the hospital she is adhering to her goal in getting them to admit to the error they had made. This not only 'puts the record straight' but also operates as a 'cleansing process.' Madeline can now move on in her life.

SELF-HELP TIPS

- Never panic and rush into quick decisions. Always think rationally and coolly about the available options.

- All crises have to be managed so that we put ourselves firmly in control.

- Crises have legacies in terms of memories. It is always important to put the record straight.

- Help is almost always available, even in the most unpredictable situations. We need to sift and sort to develop effective coping strategies.

IN THE CORPORATION

Organisations exist in a state of permanent change. They constantly face uncertainties driven by competitive pressures. These range from increasing globalisation and technological change through the need to meet changing employee expectations and needs.

This means that corporations seem to be always in crisis. This impacts upon employees since it is we who are directly affected by these crises. We are constantly having to change what we do in our jobs, to respond to new challenges and to achieve new targets. The pressures of modern-day jobs are unrelenting, creating stress, overwork and often long-term illness.

Those who have experienced major crises in their personal lives are often the best equipped to handle these challenges, for such experiences make us tough and resourceful. We refuse to accept defeat. We become resilient individuals who can handle anything that our working lives throw at us. This is why so many women who do reach the top of the corporate ladder – who gain a seat at the boardroom table – have experienced traumas in their personal lives.

CHAPTER FIVE

RHONA AND DOROTHY **Taking Decisions**

Most of us, most of the time, want to do the right thing – but what may be the right thing for you may well be 'wrong' for the people around you. For instance, could your family cope with the increased demands of that promotion you have been working towards? Should you start your own business, and risk that reliable income your family depends upon? Or spend that windfall you got on new clothes for yourself, or save it for the family holiday?

Even with only ourselves to consider, there are still times when we are indecisive, wondering whether to wear the black dress or the brown, go for a drink with friends or curl up in front of the TV, get married or stay single, go to the gym after work or pick up a calorie-laden takeaway on the way home.

A lack of confidence in ourselves and fear of failure might even lead us to procrastinate, in the hope that something or someone will make the final decision for us. A colleague of ours was fed up with his job and talked on and off for twelve years about changing his career. He eventually did so – but only after he was made redundant!

With the many decisions we have to make day in and day out, it is no wonder that we sometimes become anxious and confused, but in all of this we should not deny our ability to reason; we have it in our power to take the time we need to think quietly and honestly about what it is that we really want.

Once this is done, all we need then is the courage to go for it, sometimes with support from family and friends and sometimes alone.

RHONA'S STORY

The eldest of seven children from an Irish-Catholic family, I was brought up in Sligo, in western Ireland. I've always had a strong sense of independence and whilst I didn't really mind helping my mother look after my younger brothers and sisters, I couldn't wait for the time when I could leave home.

This got me thinking at the age of thirteen about what I was going to do when I left school, and although I wasn't exactly sure, I decided on going to university because that would at least give me a clear break from home.

My mother wasn't too pleased when I told her about my plans as she had hoped that I would stay in Sligo, work in an office and possibly get married to a local lad, as she herself had done. She had, on all accounts, been a dutiful daughter to her own mother and was disappointed that I didn't want to do the same.

I didn't like grammar school because it wasn't the school I really wanted to go to and, worse than that, I had to leave most of my friends behind. It took me a while to settle and for the first two years I wasn't particularly energetic in my studies, which I often found tedious. In the end I barely did enough to get into university where I took a degree in Sociology. A month or so after graduating with a 2:1, I got a job in Social Services.

On my first day I was taken aside by my Team Leader and warned about the dangers of becoming emotionally involved with certain cases: I must be careful about taking my work home.

Even though I welcomed the advice, I wasn't unduly concerned about that aspect of the job because I knew that I could feel strongly about things and yet not 'mither' about them. My mother was a big worrier, even over things she could, in my opinion, clearly do nothing about. To me that was pointless and in a way I think I reacted against it.

I loved the job, and after eighteen months was offered the opportunity to do a year's post-graduate course in England. My Team Leader thought it would stand me in good stead for future promotion. I accepted, not for one moment thinking that it would change my life for ever and that I would be leaving Ireland for good.

It was a few months before I was able to settle into the course in the north of England, mainly because I was missing home, friends and family and didn't much like having to live in bed and breakfast accommodation. All this changed when a fellow student found a house and persuaded me and two others to share with him.

It was at our house-warming party that I met Kevin. He had already qualified as an engineer but was taking a part-time management course. We got on well and, even though he had arrived with a few friends, they left without him, and we took the chance to spend the rest of the party together. I really enjoyed his company and we talked well into the early hours of the morning.

We saw each other a few times after that. He was married but had recently separated from his wife and so I had no qualms about dating him. Although I had had relationships before, none of them made me feel the way I did about Kevin, and before long I realised that I was very much in love with him.

About four months after we began seeing each other it came as quite a shock when I found out that I was pregnant. Although I was a little frightened and confused, I decided not to say anything about it to Kevin until I had decided on what I was going to do.

An abortion would have been an easy way out of the predicament, but since it would have transgressed my own values on life, I simply could not have lived with the guilt. Having the baby adopted was another option, and being a social worker I would know what to expect and could satisfy myself that my baby would have a good home.

I also had to consider the fact that I had an obligation to return to my employers in Ireland. They had paid my fees and some of my personal expenses, and were expecting me back at the end of the year. But I knew that it would not be easy to raise a child as a single parent in a Catholic society.

After considering the various options I decided to have the baby and to keep it.

I contacted my employers, told them of my situation and said that I would not be returning home after the course. I offered to pay back some of the money they had invested in me but my boss was surprisingly sympathetic and, after reassuring me that I did not have to repay the money, wished me good luck for the future.

My parents were hurt by the whole thing, and no doubt felt that they had failed in their efforts to provide me with a good Catholic upbringing. Of course I had lots of regrets about hurting them, and becoming pregnant outside marriage wasn't something I was proud of. But it had happened and I had to deal with it in the best way that I could.

I remember my mother telling me how unhappy she was about the whole situation, how I should have known better or should have been more careful, but I was not going to live my life by other people's prescription, not even that of my parents whom I loved dearly and who I knew also loved me. It was only after I had examined the options, and had made a decision about what I was going to do, that I told Kevin I was pregnant. This was important to me because I didn't want him to feel obligated to stay with me because of the baby. As far as I was concerned, it was my decision and if he chose to walk away I was quite prepared to bring up my child alone. In the end he simply said that he loved me and wanted us to be together as a family.

It was hard initially, because we had to find a suitable place to live and didn't have a lot of money. At first, we rented a small flat and then later, when I had found a job and a nursery for our baby daughter Kylie, we were able to afford to buy a two-bedroomed terraced house.

Kevin's divorce came through three years after we had been together, and although my parents would have liked us to get married, I didn't particularly want to. More important to me was the relationship I had with Kevin. Had I been in love with someone who shared my faith it would have been different, but Kevin was not religious and would not embrace the Catholic faith. Once again I was going against my parents' wishes, but I was secure in their unconditional love, and even though they were distressed and disappointed, and probably couldn't quite understand the decisions I made, I knew that they would always be there for me.

As a family, we were very happy until I found out that I was pregnant again. It wasn't planned, and as we were ten years into our relationship, I realised that having or not having the baby was not just my decision to make. Physically it might have been, because no man can force a woman to carry a baby, but I cared enough about Kevin to know that he also needed to be involved in making the decision about what we were going to do.

At one stage in our deliberations, Kevin asked if I would consider a termination and I said that I would. Ten years ago I would have been horrified at the thought, but my life was different now and I could not just think about my religious values and myself.

I have always been confident enough in my own values to be able to make a decision, feel sure that it is the right one, and stand by it without regret or embarrassment. On the other hand, some of my decisions were based on my religious upbringing. This one was a combination of the two and I also had to take into account how whatever I decided to do would affect the other people in my family.

Kevin and I were still very much in love with each other but we had only been together for a few months before Kylie was born. Having another child would simply be delaying the time when we could be alone to enjoy each other's company.

After much thought and discussion, the decision to have my pregnancy terminated wasn't an easy one, and not the one I really wanted to make, but the fact that it was a decision that was shared would, I thought, make it somewhat easier to live with.

Then, and almost out of the blue, Kevin said he was going to leave the decision up to me and that he would be happy with whatever I wanted to do. I don't know whether it was because he could sense how I was really feeling and I thought it best not to ask.

It wasn't hard to change my mind and Kevin and I were both extremely happy when our son, David, was born.

For years our lives continued in a contented and orderly fashion. We had two wonderful children, successful jobs that we enjoyed, and could look forward to holidays abroad. I couldn't have wished for anything more.

That was until I met Richard.

I had recently been promoted to an Assistant Director's post and had joined my colleagues on what is commonly known as 'A National Away Day', which often involved an overnight stay in some plush hotel. The event took us out of our normal environment with col-leagues of corresponding responsibility from across the country. There were also the social aspects to look forward to during the evening when drinks were normally allowed to flow freely.

Richard and I got talking about our regions and found that, although there were similar social problems, there were also many different ways of dealing with them. We both had a wealth of experiences to share.

We also talked about our families, and although he was married with three children, I was mindful of him and the way he looked and smiled at me.

It had been a long time since I had flirted with anyone, or to my knowledge, that anyone had flirted with me, and I felt a little flushed by the alcohol and the chemistry there was between us.

When the conversation began to dry up and I felt the need to control the fervour that Richard had stirred in me, I turned down his offer of another drink and wished him goodnight. He said he was sorry that I was going so soon, and suggested that we exchange business cards. The next morning we hardly spoke to each other, which I think was more out of embarrassment than anything else, and when we left after lunch I didn't expect to hear from him again.

But I was wrong, for a week later he called me at work, said he was visiting my region and wondered if we could have lunch. I was happy to hear from him and agreed to meet.

We managed some small talk before he told me that he couldn't stop thinking about me and wanted to know how I felt. I remember sipping the glass of wine I had in an attempt to steady my nerves.

How I felt was wonderful – to think that a good-looking man like Richard, someone I had met for the very first time, fancied me enough to want to see me again. In fact, it made me feel much younger than my thirty-five years!

I have always found my feelings fairly good barometers of what I should be doing, and whilst the idea of an affair brought with it a hint of excitement I knew it would not be right for me. If romance and excitement were missing from our lives, it was up to Kevin and me to do something about it. To try anything else would not only have caused some pain and long-lasting damage, it was a risk and I had too much to lose. When we said goodbye that afternoon, I knew that Richard would not be contacting me again.

My family are the most important people in my life, and I rarely make a decision outside work which does not take them into account.

My parents love Kevin and dote on Kylie and David, in exactly the same way as they do their other grandchildren. No one would have guessed that the start we had was not the kind they – and my mother in particular – would have wished for.

But on a personal level there is always a little reminder from my mother who will, whenever she gets the opportunity, take me aside to try to persuade me to at least think about getting married.

We may well get married one day, of course, but for now I see no reason to do so.

REVEREND DOROTHY'S STORY

I was ten years old when my father, a man who was very important in my life, died of cancer. He was only thirty-nine and, although I went with my mother to the funeral, I never really grieved for him until years later. He was a charismatic and popular man, and whenever my mother spoke about him she would always say how like him I was, and I was immensely proud of that.

After his death, I was surrounded by very strong women, my mother, who was a dressmaker and made fabulous evening gowns and wedding dresses, my aunts, who ran their own successful businesses as owners of shops or restaurants, and other women in our neighbourhood who were teachers or nurses.

These Caribbean women were my role models and in a way I guess they helped me to make one of my first decisions, which was that I wanted to be like them – strong and independent. They made me believe that if women were going to achieve anything in life, it had to be of their own making.

I loved school and got good grades, but even so, when it came to career choices, I was being directed into factory work, because this was what most black people did in those days, the alternative being to go into nursing. Neither of those options appealed to me and after going to college to take an administration and secretarial course, I got a job as a civil servant.

Things couldn't have been better for me. I was earning good money, living at home with my mother and having a pretty good social life. But my world almost fell apart when I found out that I was pregnant.

At first I felt ashamed of myself, as the last thing I wanted was to end up like so many other girls I knew who were living in high-rise flats with two or three kids and absent fathers. Whilst I would make sure that this did not happen to me, I was distressed by the thought that I had not only let my mother down but also myself.

Although I didn't want to be with the baby's father, because I didn't think we had a future together, I decided that I would have the child, because I was capable of looking after it. The instant relief that I felt made me realise that I had come to the right decision, and my only real worry was how I was going to break the news to my mother.

In the end I didn't have to, because she apparently sensed it, and after a few strong words on how I should have known better, and that I should have been more careful, she offered her support.

I managed well with my mother's help after Christine was born and then, quite unexpectedly, and when she was about three years old, I hit a very low period in my life and became very depressed. I felt dead inside, and although my mother tried to reach me she was unable to, nor could friends and family who wanted to help. Life suddenly held no meaning for me and although I loved Christine, I was simply going through the motions when looking after her.

I was a Christian and up until that time had been a regular church-goer, but I lost all faith and no longer wanted to go to church. In fact, I became a recluse, hardly ventured outside the house and seldom spoke to anyone. Before long, the days that I had taken as sick leave from work soon ran into weeks and then into months. Eventually my mother got me to see a doctor who promptly prescribed anti-depressant tablets.

Then one evening as I sat on the bed in my room, eleven years after his death, I could think of no one but my father. I had never really stopped thinking about him, but this time my thoughts were deeper than they had ever been before and were almost overwhelming.

I didn't much like being an only child and my father used to try and make up for that by spending as much time with me as he could. He would often say that I was a gifted child, and so when I told him that I wanted to be an actress or singer, he said that he believed that I could be both and more. I had a good voice, and whilst there were enough people who wanted to encourage me to sing Negro spirituals or reggae music, my dream was to be a Jessye Norman for she is, in my view, the greatest opera singer in the world. It appeared that only my father understood this. He was my greatest fan and I enjoyed performing and singing to him. In many ways, he enabled me to live my dreams, and looking back to when he died, it was as if all my dreams had died with him.

Feeling helplessly alone, I looked at the bottle of tablets that were on the dressing-table and thought about taking an overdose. But by some miracle, Christine, who had been asleep on the bed next to me, stirred and as I looked at her I knew instinctively that I had to be strong for her because she needed me. Fortified by that thought alone, I went straight to the bathroom and flushed the whole bottle of tablets down the toilet.

As I held Christine close to me, I suddenly realised that at the age of twenty-one, and for the first time in my life, I was actually grieving for my father and missing his love and inspiration.

I wept inconsolably as I endeavoured to relieve myself of the pain and anger that had harboured themselves inside me for years, and when there were no more tears left I decided that it was time to get on with the rest of my life. After that, I never looked back.

During my period of illness and at the time unable to see myself working again, I had left my job. Now back on my feet again but unemployed, I went out looking for work. Thinking back to all those women and my mother who had always worked, I was determined not to rely on state benefits and so I asked friends to look out for any job for me, called into different offices to ask about vacancies, scanned the local newspapers and went up to the Employment Centre at least three times a week.

My mother was very supportive and kept saying that I didn't have to rush into finding work, but it was important for my self-esteem and I wanted to make sure that Christine had all that she needed.

After a couple of weeks, I was delighted when I finally got an interview. I didn't get the job advertised but the manager was so impressed with me that he created a position for me and I started at the company as an accounts clerk.

It wasn't long before I resumed my gregarious lifestyle, and one evening when I was out with friends I met David.

We were an odd couple at first, him with dark brown hair and blue eyes, and me with my almond complexion and thick short black hair. It was the late 1960s and mixed couples were still quite a novelty at that time, and we had to be strong enough to withstand the glares and unkind remarks that were sometimes levelled against us.

We went out together for about eighteen months before David asked me to marry him. It took me a few weeks to decide because, no matter how I felt about him, I had to think long and hard about whether he was the man I wanted to spend the rest of my life with. We also had to discuss how we were going to bring up any future children and the importance of their culture and identity.

In my opinion there was little point in our children being seen as half white and half black. I was well aware of the identity issue concerning mixed-race children, and, although other people reading this may have different views, I felt it was in everybody's interest for our children to be identified as black.

At first David couldn't see the importance of this, because as far as he was concerned we were in love, our children would be born from love and nothing else should matter. In an ideal world that might well be the case, but we were far from Utopia and if we were planning on becoming parents we had to be realistic, prepared to raise our children in a manner that would make them into secure and self-confident adults.

David and I talked at length about the experiences of my mother's generation when they arrived in Britain in the 1950s, and what the future might be like for our children in a society where racism was endemic. After weeks of debate, David began to accept that our children should assume a black identity and that they would have every reason to be proud of who they were. That settled, we got married a year later and within six years, we had two boys, Nathan and Oliver.

With three wonderful children, an adoring husband, a good job and what seemed like a secure future, one would have thought that I had everything, but there was still something missing in my life.

After my depression I had regained my faith and along with it a yearning for a platform where I could use my gifts. At thirty-three, I thought it was probably too late to go to drama school, but I still had a passion for singing and joined a local opera group, became a member of the church choir and sang solos at weddings and the occasional funeral.

I also became more involved in the church, would often do the Sunday morning readings and volunteered to help with some of the administration. I enjoyed it and a few people suggested that I should become a lay preacher. The idea stayed with me for a few months and, unable to sleep one night, I suddenly realised that I had a calling to the Church and decided there and then, in the early hours of the morning, that I was going to become a priest. A surge of excitement swept over me and, unable to contain myself, I woke David and told him. He simply turned over and said, 'That is a good idea, darling, now go to sleep.'

Later that morning and after David said he thought that I had been talking in my sleep or that he himself might have been dreaming, he gave me his full support, saying that he had every confidence in me and knew that I would make an excellent priest. My family and friends were all delighted for me, and some wondered why it had taken me so long to come to that decision.

I couldn't answer that but within three months and after meetings with the bishop and attending a number of spiritual retreats with other potential candidates, I was accepted as a student of Theology and started my training.

The next three years of Biblical training and secondment to different parishes were the most fulfilling of my life, and the fact that I was going to be the first black woman priest in the Anglican Church didn't worry me at all. All I knew was that I had talent and a vocation, and that I just had to believe in myself and the rest would take care of itself.

The ceremony at which I was ordained took place when the first set of women became priests, and it was a wonderful day for my family and me. My children, David and my mother were all very proud of me and I was showered with love and good wishes from many different people.

When I took up a post in a neighbouring parish, I was more than a little nervous. After years of male dominance of one of society's most prominent establishments, there were those who still had to come to terms with the ordination of women priests, and although I was not unduly bothered by it, there were also those who had to come to terms with a woman priest who was also black.

I spent a few extra hours polishing my sermon on what was to be my first service, and as the congregation started to arrive I took a deep breath as I got myself ready to greet them. My hour, and what I knew was indeed a perfect moment in my life, had come.

David and the children sat in the front pew and I could sense their loving support. The service passed without a hitch, and I waited in anxious anticipation for the kind of response I would get as people left. Fortunately, it was all positive.

I am proud to say that decisions I have made in my life have all been based on a profound sense of belief in myself, and although they have sometimes brought sadness and disappointments, hardships even, they have also given me the sense of fulfilment and happiness that I have today.

SUMMARY

Many of us find it difficult to take decisions. We put off doing so until the decision is made for us. However, becoming pregnant requires a decision that *cannot* be endlessly deferred in the same way. Both of the above stories describe how two women found themselves pregnant and were forced to take life-changing decisions.

Rhona's story is one common to many women. All of her childhood pressures are for her to get married and stay in her local community. As she says, it is what was expected of women like her. But she has to buck the trend, to break out of the traditional role in order to lead the life she wants to have.

She leaves home and village to go to university. So far, so good. She has made a decision that stretches the boundaries of acceptable conduct as far as her mother is concerned. But then she gets pregnant. And suddenly a difficult choice has to be made. This is because there is a direct conflict between her chosen lifestyle and her personal values as shaped by her upbringing.

But she makes the decision and chooses to live with it. The result is a much more self-confident person. But she is also lucky in that she has a strong support system. There are her parents and her partner. And it is they who provide her with the criteria she uses to handle Richard. She chooses not to have an affair since she knows that to do this will destroy the trust and the loyalty that she has gained from others.

Like Rhona, Dorothy is a person who makes decisions based on rational, detailed judgement, but her case is also a typical story of someone who comes to a decision about the future direction of her life, based on an accumulation of personal experiences. We are often not clear why it is we take life-changing decisions. For Dorothy, it is the memory of her father. For years she has wanted to do something and yet there have always been factors which stopped her. Throughout the whole of her life she feels that somehow something is not quite right. And then suddenly, in the middle of the night, she realises what it is.

This is what happens to many of us. We anxiously make decisions, but somehow they do not solve the problem. In Dorothy's case it is almost as though things have decided for themselves what she should do. Some decisions cannot be 'forced'. We sometimes have to sit back and allow issues to sort themselves out.

SELF-HELP TIPS

• Never take rash, instant decisions. Think things through and, if possible, confide in others.

- Decision-making often generates tensions with others. To get them to accept the decision, their tolerance and understanding have to be stretched.

- Sometimes, introspection and self-analysis fail to offer solutions. In which case, we have to rely on our gut reactions. At the end of the day, we have to live with ourselves.

- Decisions inevitably affect other people. We have to strike a balance between our own needs and those of others.

IN THE CORPORATION

Working in business demands an ongoing process of decision-making. The person who cannot make decisions will be ineffective as a leader and manager. Decisions have to be taken about the allocation of resources, whether or not to fire a member of staff, and whether to move the business in one strategic direction rather than another.

The worst type of manager to work for is the one who cannot make decisions, the person who defers endlessly, hoping that things will sort themselves out. But they rarely do. The outcome is a business that operates rather like a rudderless ship, drifting from one uncertainty to the next.

Some people are better decision-makers than others. It is a skill which is often acquired through experience. We are forced to make major decisions in our personal lives, and, although this can cause great pain at the time, the experience gives us a resoluteness that adds to our leadership abilities. In a corporate world of constant changes, tough decisions have to be taken the whole time. Making decisions in relation to personal crises provides us with invaluable skills when sitting round the boardroom table.

CHAPTER SIX

CHARANJEET AND PEARLINE **Acting as Mentors**

When did you first realise that your child was entering adulthood?

Was it their first date, the smell of tobacco mingled with perfume, or the woollen scarf worn guardedly at breakfast in the middle of summer?

Whilst some parents may smile at the memories this conjures up, others may feel saddened as they recall the advice they gave which was ignored, the support they offered which was rejected, and the shifting allegiance to peers that took away the influence they once had.

Unprepared for these teenage challenges, you probably interfered when you did not mean to, or talked when you should have listened. These things may come back to haunt you as you think of what you might have done differently, if only you could turn the clock back, if only you had another chance.

You accompany your children along their passage to adulthood doing all that you can, but when the time comes for you to 'let go' just how sure can you be that you have done enough?

CHARANJEET'S STORY

My mother, little brother and I came to England from the Punjab when I was four years old. My father had been in Birmingham for three years before we were able to join him.

Like most other immigrants from India who came over in the late 1950s, my parents were uneducated. Dad was a manual worker in a local factory and Mum stayed at home with my brother and me and the three brothers and three sisters who followed.

We lived in an old Victorian house in the middle of Handsworth with my uncle, his English girlfriend, Jeannie, and two Jamaican families.

During the first few years of being in England I was very much influenced by the women in our house. I always looked forward to seeing the two matronly Jamaican women and hearing their exotic accents. I looked up to Jeannie, who had taken on the responsibility of looking after the whole family, and of course my mother was always on hand to instruct me on how to carry out the housework.

We hardly saw anything of my father, who I can only remember coming in from work and going out again to the pub with my uncle and the other men.

My childhood wasn't a particularly happy one, mainly because my parents were traditional Sikhs and as children we were expected to do exactly as we were told.

I was very upset one day when my mother said that the only Western clothes I could wear were my school uniform. At all other times I had to wear an Indian outfit, which was a trouser suit called a *shalmar kameez*, because I wasn't allowed to show my legs at home. My mother and I hardly spoke about anything other than the amount of housework I had to do.

I cooked, washed, cleaned and looked after my younger brothers and sisters. This left little time for me to study, but as far as my mother was concerned studying was not going to make me a good wife, and that was what my upbringing was all about.

At that time, most young Asian women went off to work in factories when they left school, but I wanted something better than that. Fortunately, I managed to get a job in an office. This only lasted for two years, after which I was told I had to have an arranged marriage.

It wasn't what I wanted, but after my parents made it clear that I had no say in the matter I married the man they had chosen for me. A few months later I was pregnant with our first child.

After having two daughters, my husband Jagdish and I were relieved to have a son, which was important to continue the family name. I then gave birth to another four daughters and was a full-time mother.

Although I took charge of the children whilst Jagdish went out to work, it wasn't easy. We lived with my in-laws for the first few years and they were forever telling me how to bring up the children. They often said that I should speak Punjabi instead of English to the children, and did not approve of me allowing them to wear Western clothes. As far as I was concerned, it was important for my children to be able to speak good English if they were to succeed in life, and as for their clothes, they wore both English and Indian so that they could, at least, have the chance to choose for themselves.

It was only when we were able to buy our own house that I really felt in control of my family.

Jagdish and I wanted our children to have a good education and so when they had to do their homework, or revise for their exams, we always made sure that they had the time, space and right environment to do so.

We were delighted when our first two children started university, but not so pleased to learn about the lifestyle of some of their student friends.

Living a moral life is vital in our culture, and, whilst I had little control over what my children did outside the home, I had impressed upon them that smoking, drinking and sex outside marriage were not acceptable in our family unit. They argued that it shouldn't matter what other people thought, but I stressed that as family members we were much more than just 'other people'. It certainly did matter.

When my eldest daughter, Kamuljit, was twenty-five, my parents and in-laws urged my husband and me to arrange a marriage for her, fearing that the longer we left it, the harder it would be for us to find her a suitable husband.

When we spoke to her about this, Kamuljit not only told us that she was not ready for marriage, but also said that she didn't want one to be arranged for her.

Although we accepted her decision, we nevertheless felt that it was important for us to say that if she met and fell in love with someone and wanted to get married, whilst we would not object, we would prefer that he was educated, had a steady job and was from the same background. With someone of a different background, she would be isolated from our community and our relatives; in particular my parents and in-laws, who held firm with tradition and would not only find it unacceptable but would probably not want to speak to her again.

Married life is enough of an effort and struggle even if you are from the same background and village. Marrying someone of a different culture or religion would be ten times worse, and so we asked her to think carefully about the consequences of such a relationship.

My middle daughter, Amarjit, says she has no intention of getting married. After her degree she plans to do her Master's and then travel. She's the most outgoing of the older children and is determined to have her own way, even if it means going against our most revered tradition.

Having long and natural hair is sacred in our Sikh religion and custom, and I took pride in looking after my children's beautiful hair. As I had often told them how important it was to recognise their hair as the asset that it is, it never occurred to me that any of my daughters would ever think about getting it cut.

But Amarjit did, and one evening she came home after school, sporting a shorter and wavy hairstyle. I was very angry and we argued about it. She was defiant and asserted that, as it was her hair, she had every right to do with it as she pleased. There could be no dispute about that, but even so I felt deeply disappointed and hurt; she had gone against my wishes on something that was so important in our culture.

A few weeks later I learned about what had led to her making this drastic decision.

When the children were growing up, they had friends from all different backgrounds but Amarjit had more white friends than the others. She was invited to all their parties and they were always welcomed in our house: if the phone rang, you could guarantee that it was for her. Then, as they all approached their early teens, I noticed that fewer friends called, and that Amarjit herself was becoming a little withdrawn. Something was wrong and I wanted to know what it was.

Although I was aware that my children were more comfortable discussing their problems amongst themselves, I always tried to let them know that I was there for them too and that they could also talk to me.

So I asked Amarjit to help me wash up after supper one evening and we talked. It turned out that her white friends had started to exclude her from some of their activities because as an Asian girl they thought she would no longer fit in with what they wanted to do Amarjit never had much interest in hanging around the streets or going into pubs and, of course, she was forbidden to smoke.

They had also made comments about the length and plainness of her hair. She had subsequently decided on a new hairstyle to prove that she could do what she wanted with it, and to try and fit in. It didn't work and she was left feeling upset and ashamed of what she had done.

Peer pressure is something most teenagers have to contend with, and as I listened to my daughter's tale of woe it was difficult not to feel partly responsible for what she was going through.

A conflict between race and culture was inevitable, and although we had raised our children in a way that we felt would enable them to fit into English society, we may not have prepared them sufficiently for a culture we ourselves had not experienced or known enough about.

I suggested that Amarjit tried talking with her friends to explain that, although she had to abide by certain rules, there were still many things that she was able to do. But she decided not to, and sought friendship from other Asian girls instead.

Like most families with children and teenagers these days, we have not escaped the keen desire for branded and overpriced goods. The older children largely accepted that we had to be careful with our finances, but the younger ones didn't like being the only pupils in their class not wearing branded trainers. In the end they asked permission to save their pocket-money, and the money they expected to get for their birthday, to buy a pair. We accepted this as a good compromise because we felt it would help to teach them the value of money.

Looking back I surprise myself at how well I coped when the children were small, going to and from school up to five times a day and doing the housework in between. The worst times were when we had three of them in nappies. We didn't have a washing machine and disposable nappies were a distant dream.

There was always a lot of juggling to do around mealtimes, particularly during the evenings after they had all showered and sat down to eat. The little ones were often very tired and it was hard work trying to make sure that they ate enough before falling asleep over their food.

At bedtimes I would tell them what were affectionately known as

'Mary Stories'. There was a moral behind each story, which taught what happened when Mary ate too many sweets, didn't tidy her room or failed to do her homework. The older children had loved these stories and wanted me to repeat them over and over again. The younger ones were indifferent and cared little about what happened to Mary!

It was important to do everything I could to stay open to all my children and to deal with whatever problems or fears they had. When my daughters were approaching puberty, I felt that it was important to talk with them about the changes that would take place. My mother never spoke with me about such things and I was left feeling terrified of what was happening to me. Preparing my daughters for this particular stage in their lives was important.

I feel fortunate to have had such wonderful children, and to have brought them up in a way that has given them much more knowledge, self-confidence and self-esteem than I ever had.

Times have changed from the old traditional and unquestioned way of life that my husband and I were reared in, and whilst we accept the fact that as our children grow older they will do certain things that we may not approve of, we nonetheless hope that they will always be aware of the standards we set and the values we hold.

We will always love our children and offer whatever guidance and support we can to them, but Jagdish and I know that when it comes to making final decisions, we will have to trust and leave it up to them.

PEARLENE'S STORY

Coming from a large family, I never planned on having just one child, but after two heartbreaking miscarriages Brian and I thought it best to be happy with our only son, Linton. However, as he grew older it became clear that Linton didn't like being an only child and it was hard for me when he kept on asking for a little brother or sister.

At the age of seven, we didn't know quite how much he understood about the reason why he was alone. How do you explain the agony of a miscarriage to a seven-year-old? And yet we could often see how upset he was about this when he had to leave friends behind after school.

Under the circumstances, and wanting the best for him, we decided to send him to St Martins, a private and weekly boarding school, where he would not only be in an excellent educational environment, but also a social and stimulating one, where he would have constant companionship with children of his own age.

Linton was a clever child and seemed to have settled well in his new school, and Brian and I were pleased with his first year's report, which told us that he was a good scholar and had achieved top grades. We were very proud of him and felt sure that we had done the right thing.

Even though we knew when Linton started at St Martins that he would be the only black child in the school, this didn't worry us too much. We felt that we could compensate for any loss of a cultural perspective by making sure that he continued to spend time with his cousins, and that we did things as a family – and that he knew about black history.

Additionally, we went on holiday to the Caribbean, ate traditional Caribbean dishes at home, tucking into fried dumplings, plantains and rice and peas and chicken, and our English was often inter-mingled with Jamaican patois. His grandparents were always telling him stories about when they were young and their adventures along the river. In this way we could be certain that he was aware of his roots and could draw self-confidence and self-esteem from them.

It was a real shock therefore when one day I went into his bedroom and saw him using white powder on his face and his arms. When I asked what he was doing, he said it was because he wanted the other children at school to stop calling him names because of his colour. I had heard of other black and mixed-race children doing these sorts of things, but had never imagined that my own son could be affected in this way.

I took the powder away and sat on the bed with my arms around him. He was crying, and for a moment I felt totally inadequate as a mother and at a loss as to what I should do. I then began to talk about the importance of being who he was, saying that he should be proud of his colour. I also reminded him that our family was made up of people from all different backgrounds and races and that we all respected and got on well with each other.

When the tears stopped, I felt able to tell him that he was as good as anyone else in the school, and had no reason to feel inferior. I offered to speak with the head teacher about the situation but Linton asked me not to, because if anyone got into trouble about it things would possibly get worse for him.

Brian was all for taking Linton out of the school, and on reflection a school with a wider racial mix would probably have been better for him, but I felt that St Martins' reputation as one of the best schools in the country would stand him in good stead for the future. As a compromise, we agreed that we would keep a close eye on him and if he became distressed again, we would move him.

In the event we didn't have to because, although we asked, Linton never told us about any more name-calling, there were no further complaints and when he left the school at eleven years old, it was with a glowing report and excellent grades.

In fact, they were good enough for him to have a choice of going to Trinity House, another fee-paying school, or the local grammar school, and in view of his initial experience at St Martins we took him to both so that he could have a say in where he wanted to go. He chose Trinity House because friends from his class were going there.

To be honest, we were pleased about this because we had learned that children who went from private to state schools often had problems fitting in.

Continuing Linton's private education, we sent him to another leading school, but one that had children from all different ethnic backgrounds. Many of them came from Africa, Asia and Europe because their parents were ambassadors for their country or visiting professionals.

The first two years were fine, but then things started to get a little difficult when Linton reached his early teens. Up until that time he would do things around the house like the vacuuming, the washing up, the ironing, and help his father in the garden. He was even motivated enough to get himself a little job working in the local hardware store. But increasingly, from his usual energetic self, I noticed that he was becoming lacklustre and even though he continued to do things they were done without conviction or enthusiasm.

When I asked if there was anything wrong at school or with his health, he would simply shake his head and say no.

Recognising the problems of adolescence, Brian and I knew that we had to be a little more patient and understanding, and hope that the values we had instilled in our son would carry him through an unsettling period.

Whilst we saw ourselves as liberal parents, we nonetheless expected Linton to conduct himself in a certain way and this meant being respectful to his peers and his elders. It was a surprise therefore when, during parents' evening, his teacher, Mr Nelson, said that he was being disruptive and not paying attention in the classroom. We were further stunned when Mr Nelson said that Linton was a big lad and that he was intimidating other students.

We could not accept this because it wasn't in his nature, and having spoken with Linton about this, we recognised that there was a clash of personality between his class teacher and himself, and were able to persuade him to bide his time until he moved up a class the next year.

Even though we knew about peer pressure and that there was always a possibility that Linton could fall into bad company, we never tried to tell him who his friends should be, although we did discourage him from staying out late at nights.

Even so, and knowing that we were never really going to be able to control what our son did when he was away from us, we were forever telling him not to be afraid to speak with us about any problems, or worries that he had.

Now I could tell that something was wrong, and, even though I was in danger of being seen as an interfering and overprotective mother, I felt it was important for me at least to try to get him to talk about what was bothering him. I couldn't, of course, *make* him talk, but I wanted him to know that the option was there if he wanted to.

He had a few friends, black and white, who used to come to the house, and when they stopped coming I asked whether they had fallen out. He simply said that one or two of them had moved away, and that he and the others were meeting up at different places. I felt there was more to this than he was saying but, not wanting to labour the point, I left it.

When I mentioned to Brian how concerned I was about Linton, he thought I was over-reacting to the fact that our son was growing up and wanted to become more independent.

But for me it wasn't as simple as that, because I could not deny the fact that in our society young black men were being subjected to stereotypes of the worst kind and I desperately wanted to protect my son from such labelling.

Rather than continue into the sixth form, Linton signed on to a college course in art and computers. He was almost seventeen and old enough to make his own decisions, and we were happy to continue supporting him.

Then one evening the phone rang and a very stern voice asked to speak to Mr or Mrs Foster. I said, 'Mrs Foster speaking,' and then listened in a kind of stupor as the person at the other end identified himself as a Sergeant Griffiths and then went on to tell me that my son Linton had been arrested and was being held at the local police station.

Seeing my distress, Brian came over, took the phone from me and noted the rest of the details. I was beside myself, and as I got into the car with Brian and we began our journey to the police station I could only think that my worst nightmare was about to begin.

It turned out that Linton had been with a group of lads who had mugged a couple in an underpass. I was very angry with him and wanted to know why he had done such a thing.

When I eventually calmed down, Linton told me that although he was with the group he hadn't done anything wrong. However, the police had decided to pick him up, along with a few others. Being in the wrong place at the wrong time cost him a spell in prison.

A sinking feeling swept over me as I tried to understand, after visiting him in prison, why my only son, who had everything going for him, a roof over his head and parents who loved and supported him, could have been caught up in such a crime.

But still, I was hoping that once he was released he would have learned his lesson and would now choose his friends more carefully and concentrate once again on his studies. Every person is allowed to make a mistake and then move on from what has happened.

Linton started back at college but, although he left the house on time every day, I found out from his tutor that he rarely attended his classes and was instead hanging around with the same lads who had carried out the muggings.

Fearing that he would end up back in prison, I was very angry with him and told him how ashamed I was of him. His father and I were trying to support him in every way and yet he was throwing it all back in our faces. I then stormed out of his room, after telling him that he should get to grips with himself.

The next morning began as normal with Brian leaving the house first and me following. I didn't see Linton before I left, and thinking that he might have been having a lie-in, or that his lectures were starting late, I didn't bother to call him.

But when I got home in the evening and went into his room, it was empty of his things – posters, shoes, and clothes. I had no idea where he had gone and began ringing around his cousins and friends, but no one had seen him.

I reproached myself for having been so hard on him, and scarcely slept that night as I wondered where he was and what might happen to him. For days I couldn't eat and at work I wasn't able to concentrate on what I was doing for any length of time before breaking down.

We were hanging on to every phone call between getting into the car and driving around looking for him. When we did eventually find him, making his way into a club with his friends, he simply said, 'I am OK, Mum and Dad. Thank you for looking after me. You have been good parents, but I now want to be on my own.'

He was now twenty years old, and, although I had known that he would leave home at some stage, I didn't want it to happen like this. I was heartbroken. Brian coped much better than I did. He told Linton that the door was always open, he could come back at any time, and that if he needed anything he only had to call.

We later found out that Linton had spent a few days sleeping on friends' floors before staying with Beatrice, my elder sister, and his cousin Mark.

I was sad that he had left, and although for a short moment I resented the fact that he preferred to be with my sister rather than with me, his mother, I was glad that he was at least safe, and I took food, money and other things to Beatrice so that she would not be short whilst looking out for him.

A few months later, Linton left my sister's place without telling anyone where he was going and ended up in prison for short periods, arrested for possessing drugs, driving without a licence, and for carrying an ice pick, which the police said was a dangerous weapon.

I believe we failed as parents, because in trying to give Linton everything he needed we spoiled him. On the other hand, some people might think that what we wanted for Linton was very different from what he may have wanted for himself.

If I had our time again, I would not have sent him to boarding school. Many people saw this as a privilege, but not Linton, and we will never really know how it affected him and set him apart from his peers.

I tried to put myself in his shoes. I knew about my culture, because I was born into it. If you are a black child born here, you are not British and you are not English. When you are at home with your family, you are safe, but when you are out in the big wide world, you don't have that sense of belonging, and there are many other pressures that you have to deal with. Some people manage and some people don't.

I try not to think about the bad times but they surface when people ask about him. Especially his grandparents, who live in the Caribbean and often want to know when he is coming to see them, or how well he is doing. I simply say that he is fine rather than upset them by telling them the truth.

Linton is now twenty-three. He calls in now and again but says little about his life. I don't know if his prison days are over and whether he is now treading a clearer path. Although it sometimes pains me to think how much he might have achieved had he not got into bad company, Linton is still our son and, whatever happens, we will never stop loving him.

SUMMARY

Mentoring is all about offering guidance and support. It is not about telling people what to do. But as mentors we are never entirely certain about the outcome of our help. As these two stories illustrate, parents can only hope to do the best for their children but ultimately it is up to the latter what they finally do.

Charanjeet's story illustrates all the best aspect of mentoring, particularly in a situation in which there is acute cultural conflict. In her case, it is a matter of managing her own preferences with those of her children. She does not give priority to one or the other. In her mentoring role, her aim is to achieve compromise. It is a matter of getting to 'Yes Yes'. She recognises that her children have their own lives to live and that these will often be in accordance with attitudes and values contrary to her own. And so she regards her task as one of providing the moral framework within which her children can make their own decisions. It is a task that requires tact, ingenuity and imagination. Mentoring demands personal assertiveness too, but without the selfish imposition of personal values on others.

There are always limits to the mentoring role. This is clear in Pearline's story. She and her partner, like most other parents, want the best for their son. They decide to send him to a fee-paying school, because it will be the best for him, or so they think. The reality is the opposite. They put him in the front line for bigotry and prejudice. He is cast into the role of outsider. He feels marginalised and even isolated, experiences that greatly affect the rest of his childhood development.

It is only when he becomes a teenager that he is able to develop his own identity independently. Unfortunately, he does so as a member of a delinquent gang.

Pearline's story suggests that she and her partner have failed in their mentoring role. This is an unfair judgement. A good intention has had an unexpected outcome. This is often the case. Mentoring is not about telling people what to do. It is about offering guidelines, advice and suggesting appropriate patterns of conduct. Whether these are acted upon is not in the gift of mentors. The practical outcomes are the results of *other people's* decisions and actions.

SELF-HELP TIPS

- Never have fixed expectations of mentoring outcomes. This is not a responsibility of mentors.

- Offer only guidance and support. Mentoring is not about telling people what to do.

- Mentoring almost inevitably involves conflicting values, goals and aspirations. Mentoring is about what is best for the other person rather than what we *think* is best for them.

- As mentors, never impose personal wishes, values and ambitions.

- Tolerance and understanding are the bedrock of successful mentoring. Without these, no advice will be regarded as acceptable and legitimate.

IN THE CORPORATION

Mentoring is becoming an increasingly important managerial responsibility. Our jobs are constantly changing in some uncertain business environments. Education and formal training can no longer provide us with all the skills we need to be effective in our jobs.

In many organisations we, as employees, are left to sort ourselves out and to work out our own solutions. This causes stress, anxiety and inefficiency. Mistakes are made, often because we are not shown how to do things properly.

The modern manager is a team leader. In this role, it is his/her responsibility to work alongside colleagues and to offer guidance and direction. This does not mean telling other people what to do, which only causes resentment and hostility. It is a matter of guidance, of pointing colleagues in the right direction and suggesting how they can do things better.

Effective mentors are highly respected. They are regarded by their colleagues often as the source of knowledge and innovation. They are treated as trusted friends who can be turned to and relied upon always to offer guidance and support when problems arise.

Unfortunately, the culture of too many organisations encourages autocratic control rather than the creation of mentor-based support systems. But even in these, the ultimate responsibility for what we do rests with ourselves. We should never blame our mentors for our own mistakes. An effective mentor is trustworthy and supportive, key features for anyone who applies for entry to the corporate boardroom.

CHAPTER SEVEN

ABENA AND DULCIE **Building Teams**

In today's busy society we very often have to rely on our families, friends or other people, to help us achieve the goals we set for ourselves. We are grateful to the neighbour who looks after the house when we take a holiday, the babysitter who allows us that night out, or the friend who is there to help us over that painful relationship. Throughout our varied experiences, we would do well to surround ourselves with people whom we trust and know will not let us down.

In many ways, this is the kind of teamwork which can be expressed through our everyday actions – at home, at work, or at leisure, and at times when we are creating, delegating, negotiating and collaborating. We are social beings and our sense of belonging often comes from our being part of, or contributing to, something in a way that provides opportunities for mutual learning, sharing and supporting.

No longer seeing ourselves as individuals and having it all to do, but as equal and respected members of a team, we can achieve much more in ways that can save us time and a lot of energy.

As there are enough platitudes to suggest that 'no one is an island', or that 'many hands make light work', let's find out just how good you are at getting the most out of your workmates, family or the people around you.

ABENA'S STORY

It is not unusual in certain parts of Ghana for children to be brought up by older siblings and so, when at the age of nine I was told that I had to go and live with Esi, one of my older sisters, I was thrilled.

Esi, who had recently got married and moved to another town, was the youngest of four wives who were married to a polygamist – which is not illegal in our country. As all the other wives already had children and had formed relationships with each other, Esi needed companionship and I was able to provide it. In return she had to look after me, made sure that I went to school, paid my fees, and bought my clothes.

Our community was clearly divided along gender lines whereby women assumed traditional roles of caring for family and children, and men were the main breadwinners. It was therefore left to Esi to teach me all the things she felt I needed to know to become a good housewife. I didn't worry too much about this at the time because I loved my sister and saw the chores I was given as a fair return for all that she was doing for me.

At university I developed very strong views about how women were being treated in our society. Female circumcision was common practice, carried out by people with no medical background who would often use contaminated instruments. A few women bled to death because of this and I became part of a women's group that spoke out against this barbaric practice.

Although Esi cautioned me against my apparently 'feminist tendencies', which she said would not fit with what was expected of me, I was determined not to be shackled by traditions. But this all changed when I met my husband Ocansey.

We were from neighbouring villages, and our families, who knew each other, were eager for us to get married. We did so a year after Ocansey qualified as a chemical engineer and I had finished my degree in Business Administration.

For the first few months of our marriage, we lived with my in-laws where I was nothing more than a glorified housekeeper. It was what was traditionally expected of me, and with no other form of support I had little choice but to get on with the washing, cleaning, cooking and anything else that my in-laws felt needed to be done.

This went on for about six months until Ocansey, who worked for a multinational chemical company, got a post in England. Within months we were living in London and I was pregnant with my first child.

Shortly after the birth of our daughter Armina, my in-laws thought it was a good time to come and spend some weeks with us. I didn't object, but once again found myself having to wait hand and foot upon them in spite of the fact that I also had a baby to look after.

In no time at all I was back to the nightmare I had been forced to endure just after my marriage. This time, I really couldn't manage but felt that I had to, if only to prove that I was a good enough wife and mother, and not to cause embarrassment for Ocansey.

But it was impossible to keep going and eventually, after weeks of drudgery, I became quite ill. It all happened one afternoon when I suddenly felt unsteady on my feet and collapsed. I was taken to the casualty department of our local hospital and, after a number of tests and routine examinations, was told that I was suffering from sheer exhaustion. The only cure was rest, and I needed lots of it.

That was the first major lesson I learned about trying to live up to expectations, rather than admitting that I needed help from the people around me. Deciding that I never wanted such an experience again, I told Ocansey that whilst his parents would always be welcome in our home, both he and they would have to share some of the responsibilities.

Ocansey, who had been extremely worried about my health, agreed with me and began doing the main shopping at weekends. He helped with other chores and sometimes, when his schedule allowed, did some of the cooking. This would be unheard-of back in my village in Ghana, but with the demands of modern life in England we simply had to work as a team.

Within the next ten years I had another two children, Lydia and Adjie. More used to my surroundings and having made friends with other young mothers in my neighbourhood, I was in a much better position to manage my young family. But I wasn't going to do it alone because the children were of an age when they could help.

I gave them little things to do around the house, which ranged from putting things away neatly when they were not being used, to clearing the dinner-table and helping with the washing-up.

At first there were plenty of arguments as to why they should have to help with the housework when most of their friends did not. I explained to them that, as members of the family, they were expected to do their bit to make sure that the house was kept in a tidy state, especially if they wanted to invite friends to come round.

Most of their chores were organised for the weekend so as not to interfere with their homework during the week. But things did not always go to plan, particularly when some had been given easier tasks, like emptying the bins, whilst others had harder ones, like cleaning the bath. Although I explained that chores were given out on the simple basis of what needed to be done, Armina was not convinced. She was adamant that she had been given more to do than the others because she was older, and thought this unfair because she wasn't spending any more time in the house than they were.

Both girls thought that Adjie had less to do because he was a boy.

Rather than prolong the arguments, I suggested that we organise a rota so that each had a turn at doing everything. They all agreed and so we made a list of what needed to be done and planned around that.

On some occasions I had to supervise the children as they carried out their tasks, and when they did well, or if there was extra work that needed to be done, like when we were expecting visitors, they were given a little extra pocket money.

The things they did were not always perfect – for example, you could often see less in the bathroom mirror than before once Lydia had cleaned it, and there was always one little bin that Adjie had forgotten to empty, but as long as they were making a genuine effort, I was satisfied.

As one would expect, our situation was constantly changing as the children grew up. By the time Armina was a teenager, two significant changes had taken place: I had passed my driving test (after three attempts!), and Ocansey had been promoted to a national position in his company, which meant plenty of travel around the country and even short periods abroad.

The feeling of liberation caused by having my own little car only lasted until I realised that I had entered into a whole new ball-game when the girls started to get involved in after-school activities and I was having to ferry them from one place to the next.

Not wanting to be left out, Adjie too started his after-school football sessions, which was problematic at first as it clashed with Lydia's dance sessions on Tuesday afternoons. In the end, we were able to juggle the times, deciding that Lydia would have to wait an extra twenty minutes before she was picked up.

Even though I seemed to spend the evenings running a non-profit-making taxi service, I still had plenty of free time in the day and, wanting to make the most of that time, I began to do some voluntary work with an organisation for homeless young women. It was great to be able to resume my interest in women's issues and it was even more rewarding to know that I was helping many of the young women who came into the Centre to get their lives back in order.

A few months after I had started my voluntary work, a part-time position came up at the Centre and, although I was being encour-aged to apply for it, I first had to discuss it with the family because it was bound to affect our routine. Although the children were great about it, saying that it was better than me being stuck in the house all day long, Ocansey was less forthcoming. His main concern was about Adjie, as any afternoon shift would mean that I would be half an hour late in picking our son up from school. However, this didn't stay a problem for too long. Luckily Carole, the mother of Adjie's best friend, stepped in and offered to help. Arrangements were made for her to pick Adjie up and keep him in her house until I collected him on my way home.

I got the job, loved every minute of it and felt that I was on my way to the independence I had promised myself back in Ghana.

By this time, the girls in particular were going through a phase of wanting to be more with friends than family. 'Sleepovers' at friends' houses were happening on a regular basis, and this meant that weekend chores were either being left until during the week, or else not being done at all. Whilst this wasn't a problem initially, it started to become a good excuse for the children, and particularly Armina, who was going to more 'sleepovers' than anyone else, to get out of doing their chores.

Not surprisingly it was Lydia, the most argumentative of all the children, who said that this was unfair and that she didn't see why she should have to continue with her work whilst Armina was able to get away without doing hers.

Once again, this called for a compromise, and I suggested that they could either organise themselves to cover each other's chores, or someone could do two weeks in a row. But whatever they decided to do, it was up to them to make sure that the tasks got done.

A week or so later a major argument erupted because Lydia, after promising Armina that she would clean the bath for her on a weekend that she was going to be away, failed to do so. Armina, fuming and no doubt suffering from a little adolescent 'paranoia', was convinced that Lydia had done this on purpose to get her into trouble with their father or me.

When both girls had calmed down, I was able to explain to Lydia that if she had agreed to help Armina by doing her chore she should have kept her word. It was a matter of trust and reliability, and Armina was understandably feeling very let down.

Lydia apologised and said that she had genuinely forgotten to do the bath because she had done it the week before.

But even more apologies were needed when Adjie missed his friend's birthday party by a whole two hours.

In my experience, and I am sure that other parents feel the same, communication is not always at its best with teenagers. You can tell them one thing and they either interpret it differently or dismiss it altogether.

On this particular occasion Adjie was due to attend a birthday party that was being held in a restaurant. We arrived at 3.00 pm, just in time to see everybody putting on their coats. We had received a phone call to inform us of the change in time but thanks to Lydia, who had taken the message, Adjie had still missed the party. He was inconsolable and rightly annoyed with his sister, who had first failed to pass on the message and then, to compound his anger, had passed it on incorrectly.

We were only able to bribe Adjie into submission with a promised special visit to the same restaurant with his friend and a few others. It was a costly compromise, but it was the only way of ensuring that peace would prevail in our house.

When I look back, it was probably a good job that I fell ill so early in my marriage. It taught me a valuable lesson that I other-wise might not have learned for many years; and that was to make sure I got the support I needed from my children, husband and other people like Carole. I didn't mind being in charge of keeping a good home and family, as long as everyone else played their part.

DULCIE'S STORY

As the youngest of five girls being brought up in Jamaica in the 1940s, my mother used to say that I was the little boy she never had because I was always hanging around the streets with the boys and enjoyed doing everything they did.

When my mother wanted me to join the Brownies, I wanted to join the Scouts; when she sent me to dancing sessions, I would go to the boxing club instead to spar with the boys who were there. I loved sports and would play any game that was in season, whether it was cricket, football or even kite-flying.

Whenever there was a sports event in our little town, nothing could keep me away. At the age of twelve I especially enjoyed going to the cycling track on Friday evenings when competitions were being held. I didn't have any money to get in and so used to stand next to the fence round the stadium with lots of other people and watch. My mother would forbid me to go but I would sneak out as soon as I got the chance to do so.

I kept this up for years until I was sixteen and was able to pay to get into the stadium. That's where I met my husband, Stanley. He was a professional cyclist and I had been watching a championship event when he came over and started talking to me. He then asked me where I lived and I gave him the wrong address because I wasn't interested in having a boyfriend at the time. But Stanley was persistent, and we went out together for about three years before his family decided to emigrate to England.

Stanley stayed in touch after he got to England through letters and the odd, short telephone conversation because it was so expensive to call long-distance.

Then one day when I arrived home my mother said a telegram had come for me. She had signed for it and I could tell straight away that it was from Stanley. I was worried at first, thinking something awful might have happened, but when I opened the telegram, it was an invitation from his parents saying that they wanted to send for me to join them in England.

At first I wasn't interested in going to England, because I had a good job and was happy at home. But my mother and sisters thought it was too good an opportunity to miss.

We stayed with Stanley's parents for a little while until we were able to get our own place. Stanley got a job in the factory where both his parents worked. I tried to get a job in a printing office but in those days West Indians were not considered suitable for office jobs.

I decided that I wanted to train to become a nurse, but when I was told that I had to live in the nurses' home Stanley wasn't too happy about us having to be apart and so, feeling disillusioned, I gave up looking for work and we decided to start a family.

I eventually had three children, Joel, Morris and Charlene, and I became a full-time mum.

We lived on an inner-city housing estate and with hardly anything for the kids to do I used to be out on the playing-fields teaching them how to play football. All my children enjoyed playing sports, and both Joel and Morris were particularly good at football. Joel, who was the eldest, had the chance to play for a local team, but his father felt that it was better for him to concentrate on his schoolwork and he did so. Morris on the other hand was stubborn like me, and not even threats from his father could put him off playing football. In the end, Joel went off to university and Morris went on to sign for Manchester United.

All the lads enjoyed playing football during the week after school and at weekends and I was very much involved with the team, organising refreshments, providing lifts to and from away games and even washing and ironing the kits. They started when they were around eleven years old and went right through their secondary education together, winning many trophies on the way. Not wanting to give up entirely after leaving school they asked Sammy, who was a youth-worker, and me if we could keep the team going. We agreed and within a few weeks Woodstock FC was formed.

Because some of the lads were sixteen or seventeen we entered them into the open league, where they came across older men who whipped them every time they played. That's when Gerald, the captain, asked if we could do some extra training. The other lads were not keen at first, but, realising that if they didn't train they wouldn't improve and were likely to be beaten every weekend, they decided that they should have training sessions.

They could sometimes be mischievous and a little unruly and, whenever they got the chance, would often wind up Sammy who always appeared to be living on his nerves. Sammy didn't like being teased and I had managed to talk him out of leaving the club on a number of occasions. But after the last prank, he decided that he had

had enough and not even I, whom he trusted, was going to be able to convince him to stay this time.

It so happened that one Sunday when we were about to go for a match, Sammy had forgotten something and had to go back to the youth club to get it. We were all waiting in the mini-bus for him and by the time he returned, one of the lads, Winston, who was a midfielder and lively on and off the pitch, was sitting in his seat. Sammy asked Winston to get out of his seat. Winston kept pretending not to hear what he was being asked to do and with the others laughing and jeering, Sammy simply picked up his stuff and got off the minibus.

The other lads were in an uproar and went mad at Winston, saying that he should go after Sammy. I tried to calm them down and then one of them asked if I could drive the bus. I could and did, and once we got to the grounds, I also signed up as the coach. Even though we lost the match, it was the start of my football-coaching career.

Throughout my years of playing football in Jamaica and watching how the training and coaching sessions were being conducted I felt confident that I could run the team and started by devising a programme for the lads so that they could improve their level of fitness.

I organised training sessions for them that included a weekly trip out to the Lickey Hills, which was a popular country park. I would drop them off at the bottom of a hill, which they had to run up, and then drove the mini-bus round to the other side, where they would then meet me.

The first time we tried it at the Lickeys I thought they had all got lost because it took them such a long time to get to where I was waiting for them. When they eventually arrived, one after the other, I found out that, far from running, they had all decided to walk and were moaning about feeling weak and tired. But at least they all made it and to me this showed a good level of commitment.

As time went on, whilst some people started to train properly others didn't, and so we were knocked out of the cup games in the early rounds and lost most of our league games in the first year. This made people realise that if they wanted to win they would have to take training more seriously and so at last, and no matter the weather, everybody started to turn up and work hard.

This paid off and the next year we started to win everything and became the Manchester United of the Birmingham Sunday League.

Even so, things were not always perfect and I constantly had to nag the lads about their time-keeping. When I threatened to leave them behind if they were late, they would only laugh at me, saying I would be letting the team down. A lad called Peter Horton was the worst. He was a midfielder and a very good player, and the team relied on him a lot.

One Sunday, after waiting for over twenty minutes for him I decided that we had to go. The lads were creating a din, saying that we would lose the game without him and if we did it would be my fault. Well, I told them that if they lost the game, they would have to blame *themselves* because one person alone didn't make a team and it was up to all of them to try and win, and they did. Peter, who until that time had thought that he was invincible and that the team could not win without him, suddenly changed his attitude and started to turn up on time, especially when he had to work hard to get his place back.

We had a squad of fifteen and there was always a problem when I had to take players off. Even though we had a rota they didn't like it and would moan at me, saying I didn't know what I was doing, I wasn't a good enough coach, and even refusing to play for the team again. But if we were winning, as we often did, I felt that it was right to give other lads a go, even if they were not as good as the ones I had taken off. They needed the experience and I needed to build and strengthen the team.

One of the hardest things for me was to instil discipline in the team because a few of the lads were hot-headed and would sometimes argue with the referee. Whenever this happened, we would have to pay a fine and, for a club that was already struggling to find fees, this wasn't a particularly clever thing for them to do.

But sometimes I had to control myself, especially when an unfair decision was made against us. There was a lot of racism around at that time and the team, which was all black, felt that decisions went against them because of this.

There was one time when a member of another team kicked one of our boys on the back of his legs and the referee, who the other team had chosen, did not penalise the lad who had done it, although it was a clear foul. Our lads surrounded him, whilst another one was going head to head with the culprit at the other end of the pitch.

One of our players was sent off and I was angry at the lad who had head-butted the chap who committed the foul because he lost us the game. But I was also furious with the referee, and some of the lads had to help calm me down. Although I wanted to, I didn't argue with the referee because as manager of the team I knew that I had to set an example. Instead I used the channel that was open to me by writing a letter of complaint to the league. It didn't change anything, but at least I felt better.

Most of the lads were either at college or on the dole because they couldn't find work, and this meant that quite a few of them couldn't pay their subs or contribute to the registration fee, which was over £200.

Money was also needed to pay the referee, for the grounds and to affiliate to the governing body, and so we started to take money from the ones who could afford to pay and leave the others who couldn't.

After a little while this proved problematic, with some lads arguing about having to subsidise others, especially if they didn't get to play a full game. In the end we decided that everyone should pay a little, and this was set at a level which they could all afford.

By this time I had found a job as a youth-worker, and I was able to use some of my wages to run the team. Sometimes I even had to loan the lads a few pounds to get personal things. Most of the time they paid me back, but it didn't always matter if they didn't: what was important for me was that they were able to concentrate on playing the games without having to fret about where their next meal was coming from.

The club has been going for nearly twenty-five years now, and as well as my son, Morris, can boast a few semi-professional and professional players, some of whom signed for big clubs and went on to play for England and one for Jamaica in the World Cup Finals in France.

I think that if you are into something you love, you want to do it well.

I had no formal training to become a football coach, but I could play the game. I observed and picked up as much as I could from the PE teacher who used to take the school football team, I watched the game on television, would listen to the commentary and made sure that I was up to date with the rules.

I also have the respect of the team, and, even though some of the lads can be difficult at times, I know that they respect me, and the decisions I have to make.

Now in my sixties, and with a squad of twenty-five and younger ones coming up all the time, I can't think of anything better than being out there with the boys and doing what we all enjoy best, playing football.

SUMMARY

We are all, in one way or another, involved with teams. Sometimes this can be inside the home. On other occasions, it is because of our jobs, working relationships or leisure activities. These two stories demonstrate the importance of teams for personal development.

Abena is brought up in a country where women's labour is cheap and exploited. It exists for the needs of men and other family members. There are no opportunities for her to develop her own talents or for her to organise her life as she wants to.

It is only after moving to England and falling ill through sheer exhaustion that she realises that she must cut down on her workload. She does this by making her children work as a team. She creates a division of labour in which each child has to pull their own weight. Through this, a set of expectations is established for each team member. It becomes 'self-managed' through which everyone is able to achieve their own goals.

This allows Abena to devote some attention to herself. Instead of being burdened down through working for others, she manages the team so she has time for herself. As in all teams, there are disputes and disagreements. It is Abena's responsibility to settle these to everyone's satisfaction.

Her story demonstrates how we can best meet our own needs by working with and through others. If we all selfishly pursue our own interests, the outcome is individual competition and the exploitation of those with goodwill. In fact, no one benefits in the long term.

Dulcie's is a rather different story but with a similar lesson. She is addicted to sport as a child and in later years finds herself as a coach to a local football team. Her organising skills are tested to the full as she manages a group of highly individualistic, competitive young men.

She finds that she has to set standards of conduct and impose discipline about having training sessions and turning up to play games. Egos have to be managed and discipline has to be imposed. On top of all this, she has to find funds to pay for travel, Football Association fees and so on. But in the end, she creates a winning team against all the odds.

But there is also something in it for Dulcie. She acquires skills that she can use for her own personal development. By acting as team coach she gains an understanding of young people and how to get the best out of them. She becomes a youth-worker.

SELF-HELP TIPS

- Team leaders need to be assertive and always able to keep control.

- Managing disputes and the ability to resolve tensions is an essential feature of the team leader's role.

- There will always be team members with inflated egos. Spot them early and manage them closely. They can easily destroy team morale and therefore team performance.

- All team members need to know what is expected of them if they are to perform well. Defining and allocating roles, then making sure that these are undertaken, is a key responsibility of team leaders.

IN THE CORPORATION

In the old days, organisations acted as machines. Each of us was expected to behave as a predictable cog in these well-oiled machines. We were given precise role descriptions with exact details of what we were supposed to do and how to do it. The organisation consisted of a neat complex of clearly defined duties and responsibilities. It was the duty of line managers to organise and to supervise these arrangements. There was a strict hierarchy of control, with each person reporting to another through a military-style line management structure.

Today's organisations have to be adoptive and flexible. They face constant changes in their business environment requiring rapid decision-making and highly responsive operational procedures. It means that, instead of working according to useful job descriptions, we have to be highly flexible and capable of working with others in teams.

Managers now have to be team leaders. They have to be able to inspire and to motivate. They have to have the ability to build and maintain teams among colleagues who are often highly competitive and very individualistic. Conflicts have to be managed and disputes resolved. Awkward individuals have to be moulded into co-operative team members. Team morale has to be managed to generate high performance.

To be successful in the modern corporation, leadership skills are absolutely vital. Unless we are able to excite and to generate enthusiasm among our staff, we are not going to see high performance. Those who, through their personal experiences, become team leaders are the ones most likely to be knocking on the door of the corporate boardroom.

CHAPTER EIGHT

MARIE-HENRIETTE AND SYLVIA **Managing Time**

Management books will often tell you that if you are in control of your time you are in control of your life – having the time to do the things you like doing, staying on top of your work and achieving that much-talked-about 'work–life balance'.

Yet the reality is, in this age of modern technology which promised us so much more leisure time, there are further demands on us to go to meetings, to increase our workload, to work till late, and to put off retiring or even to come out of retirement.

But sooner or later we have to stop and think about our time – how we use it, how we invest it, and to whom we give it – or we won't know if we are getting the financial and emotional returns we hope for.

The words 'planning' and 'discipline' come to mind, because they invariably help us to decide what it is that we have to do, and give us the control to do it. But if it's as easy as this, why do so many of us wonder about where time is going, or bemoan the amount we some-times waste?

More to the point, how would you go about juggling paid work, housework, partner, children, family and friends – and still have time to achieve the goals you set for yourself?

MARIE-HENRIETTE'S STORY

I came to England from Paris in 1953 to be an au pair and to learn English. I was young and ambitious and it didn't take me long to settle with a family in Birmingham and to register on an English course at Birmingham University.

My classes were in the evenings and I would sometimes stay behind when they were over to socialise with friends at the University Centre. It was during one of these occasions that I met my first husband, Albert, who was also a student and studying to be an engineer.

There was strict immigration control in those days and so I had to return to Paris after a year. But Albert and I stayed in touch and he came to see me a few times in Paris before eventually asking me to marry him. A year later, we got married in my hometown of Burgundy.

When we returned to England, I became a housewife, had my first child a year later and three more children within six years.

Even though the housework kept me busy, the children always came first, and it was never a problem for me to shift priorities as far as they were concerned. For example, if I had planned to do something at home but saw that the weather was good, I would forget whatever it was that I was going to do, make a picnic and take the children to the park. To me, it was more important for them to be out and enjoying the sunshine, because whilst I had control over the housework, I had absolutely none over the weather and so had to make the most of it whenever I could.

With Albert working full-time, and four children – Michael, Philip, Peter and Candice – to look after, I had little time to think about myself. But my reprieve would come each summer when we went home to Burgundy. We would spend up to a month there each time, and as my mother was keen to take over the cooking and everything else, I took the time I had to relax, soak up the good weather and enjoy the beautiful countryside with the family.

At home in England, the children were very good and often wanted to help around the house with the cleaning, washing and especially with the cooking. It was of course much quicker for me to do things myself, but it was time well spent because I was teaching them some of the practical things in life, and when I needed some help they were very useful.

After ten years of marriage, Albert and I separated. We had been drifting apart for some time and I never really knew whether it was my preoccupation with the children that had started it.

A year after my divorce came through, I met and married my second husband, Edward, and had two more children, Martin and Collette. Edward was a self-employed product designer, had his office at home and was able to help with the children.

As you can imagine, our house was a very busy one, especially when the children and their friends were coming in and out and Edward had to meet his clients. But even so, we still found time to socialise and to entertain friends. I loved cooking and prided myself on my traditional French cuisine. Friends enjoyed the meals and, knowing that we didn't have a lot of money, would sometimes pay towards the cost of the food.

This went on for years, and then one evening, after a particularly appetising meal, Mina, who was a close family friend, suggested that I should think about opening a restaurant.

By this time the older children were teenagers and, having seriously thought about making a career for myself, the idea of a restaurant had an instant appeal and I decided to try it.

Eighteen years after first studying in England, I was back at night school again. Only this time it was at the College of Food and I was taking a course in cookery and food hygiene.

Edward was very supportive and not only looked after the children whilst I studied, but also helped me to draw up a business plan. Within a few months we had found a little place which had been a transport café, and took over the lease for a year.

Friends and family were around to help with decorating the place, Edward got on with the design and layout, and I was responsible for buying the equipment and the furniture. A few months later, our little restaurant, which we called 'Le Copper Kettle', was ready for its first customer.

Business was slow at first and it was mainly friends who supported us, but as word got out about the first 'authentic' French restaurant in town, we began to attract new customers.

As more people came along and we were looking for money to invest in the business, I remembered my husband's accountant saying that businesses most prone to bankruptcy were ones like ours and those in the building trade. If that wasn't enough to put us off, he then added that the price of coffee was going up! But this didn't discourage me, because as far as I was concerned it was a matter of us planning to buy sensibly and selling at a price that would make a profit. With this in mind, I often went to the wholesale market which was open from four o'clock in the morning but I wouldn't get there until an hour before it was due to close when I knew that the market-traders were more likely to barter and I could get some good bargains. But even more important, with fewer people to serve, you had time to build up a relationship with traders, and many of them were inclined to share ideas about how to cook certain dishes. I learned a lot from them.

It wasn't long before we had a thriving business and were able to employ a number of students from the university as waiters and waitresses. I supervised their training and one of the things I used to say to them was that they should always be using their eyes, ears and hands. They should be looking to see if a customer needed their attention, listening carefully to what the customers were ordering, and they were not to return to the kitchen to place an order without taking something with them, like an empty plate, or surplus cutlery. These were little things, but they all saved time.

On a personal level, I was always looking to use time more efficiently, especially around busy periods like Christmas, and would prepare my sauces the night before and put them in the refrigerator for the next day. Some of the chefs who worked with me were surprised that I did this, because they felt that everything should be freshly made. However, I was able to convince them that not only would it give us the extra time we needed to provide a better service to our customers, but that, left standing, the ingredients would marinate and the sauces would develop more flavour.

It was about this time that Peter, my eldest son, decided that he wanted to go into catering as a career so now I could combine my duty to the family with working closely with him, delegating to him tasks I didn't have time to do myself and teaching him what I knew about running a restaurant. Again, although it took a bit more time to do some things as I had to explain them to Peter, it was time well spent as increasingly he was able to take responsibility for a wider range of tasks. I was happy to work with him and he was keen to learn as much as he could. I looked forward to the day when I could take time off and leave the running of the restaurant in family hands. This day was to arrive sooner than expected.

As we extended our repertoire of recipes, we began to serve dishes like coq au vin, boeuf bourguignon and entrecotes, and it was when the tables were being fully booked, week after week, that we decided to expand.

It took us a little while to find a suitable place and then, just as we were about to sign the contract, I was involved in a very serious road accident.

I was driving home from the restaurant one evening when another car ran into the side of me. My car was a write-off and it apparently took hours for the firemen to cut me from the wreckage. I had fractures of the pelvis, broken ribs and internal injuries, and remember coming in and out of consciousness with excruciating pain and knowing instinctively that I was lucky to be alive.

After an emergency operation, I was admitted to the intensive care unit and remained there for two weeks because I needed a respirator to help me breathe.

When I was eventually moved to a ward I started physiotherapy almost immediately, and it seemed unreal to think that within three weeks I could have gone from being a healthy, active, independent and successful businesswoman to someone who had to spend time re-learning things I had once taken for granted like walking, or simply raising my hand.

When I was first taken out of bed and put to sit in a chair, feeling weak and crippled with pain, I begged the nurses to put me back in bed but they said it was the only way I was going to get stronger. When I did manage to get put back to bed, I was surprised to know that I had only been sitting out for about five minutes. The intense pain made it seem like hours.

As I began to feel better, it was hard for me to come to terms with the fact that my time was no longer mine to do with as I pleased, and that I was dependent on other people to look after me: the nurses who had to wash, dress and feed me and sit me in the chair at their discretion; the doctors who came to examine me with an entourage of medical students in tow, and the physiotherapist who would put me through what started as gentle exercises but soon turned into more rigorous ones, whether I was up to it or not. But this was no time for self-pity, I was alive and this alone was enough to help me deal with the frustration and feelings of hopelessness.

Edward visited every day and the children, friends and other family members came intermittently. Although it was good that people wanted to see me, I would have preferred using the time I had to rest, especially as it was sometimes hard having to listen to everyone talking about what they were doing, when all I could really talk about was bedpans, irritating patients who kept me awake at nights, and very poor hospital food!

Although the medical staff feared that I would be left paralysed from the waist down, I was determined to walk again and took my first steps with the help of a walking frame.

Within three months I was able to make my way to the patients' day room, could sit for long periods and kept myself occupied with card games, and flicking through magazines and recipe books because I could not concentrate long enough to read books. I read my get-well cards and letters, some of which unfortunately complained about the meals at the restaurant, which they said had dropped in standard since my absence.

I had given little thought to the restaurant, which was being run by my son, Peter, who was still training to be a chef. The letters were devastating, and although I was bothered by my constraints, at least I had plenty of time to think about what I was going to do with regard to the business, which appeared to be on the verge of collapse. In the end, I decided that it would be best to sell 'Le Copper Kettle', continue with the purchase of the other premises, but not open it as a restaurant until I had fully recovered and could go back to work.

After learning that I would probably have another two months in hospital, I decided to use some of that time to make plans for the new restaurant, and to work with Edward on the layout and design. I was already determined to get back to full fitness again, but the idea of going back to a new and much larger restaurant gave me the impetus to improve even more. As I lay in hospital I would visualise menus, table layouts, the design of the kitchen and all the other things that I knew I would have to organise when I got out.

Six months after leaving hospital, our new restaurant was ready to open but, as I couldn't cope with all that I was doing before, I decided that it would be best for me to prepare the ingredients we needed for the dishes we had on the menu. Although my son, who had by this time qualified as a chef, did most of the cooking, being blessed with a good palate I could tell with the tiniest of tastes whether a little more garlic, or a drop of wine, for instance, was needed to develop the flavour of the food.

A week before we opened, a friend of mine who worked for a local newspaper ran an article with pictures of the new place, and before long our old customers were back and we managed to attract a number of new ones.

Looking back to when I was on my hospital bed, the thought never once occurred to me that I would not be able to go back to the business. I was also pleased that the time I had spent with my children and particularly Peter, teaching them how to cook, select and buy good food and organise kitchens and tables had been well spent.

Peter now runs his own restaurant in France, my next son Michael has taken over the running of the restaurants we have opened in Birmingham, and now Edward and I can enjoy the luxury of spending more time together at home or in France. That is not to say, however, that I just let them get on with it – after all, it is a family business and it is still my name at the top of the menu! And I do so enjoy teaching my grandchildren how to set out tables and to wash up properly!

SYLVIA'S STORY

Working in public relations and marketing, time is the most valuable thing that I can give to my family, my employees and myself, and I am grateful to my mother for having given me the discipline to use it well.

She is my role model because it was tough having to bring up my four sisters, my little brother and me by herself when my father left us, and she did a great job.

On weekdays we were all very organised. Glenda and Beryl, my elder sisters, were up first with my mother between 6 a.m. and 6.30 a.m. to help prepare breakfast and lunch and to get themselves ready for work and college. Then it was Carol and I because we were next in age at nine and eleven. Washed and dressed, we had to help with the youngest two, Andrea who was seven and Peter who was four.

It was a fairly strict regime and so, even if we were awake, we would not get out of bed until we were called. Sometimes I would lie in bed, listening to the clattering of pots and pans in the kitchen, my sisters' and mother's chatter and muffled music and what sounded like news reports from the transistor radio. As the time approached 7.30, I would anticipate my mother opening the door to the stairs, and then calling, 'Sylvia and Carol, it's time!' It was always my mother who called us, and how I looked forward to hearing her voice first thing in the morning.

Nowadays, married, with a demanding job as a Marketing Director, and a seven-year-old son, Christopher, my day begins at 7 a.m. to the sound of an alarm clock.

Frank, my husband, who works shifts, leaves the house at 7 a.m. or comes home after a night shift, when we have already gone, and so I have sole responsibility for getting Christopher ready and taking him to school. Whilst he will get up and shower without any trouble, Christopher takes for ever over his breakfast and so the extra time I build in for him to finish eating I also use for myself.

In my job, my appearance is important, and so my hair, face, clothes and nails all have to look good. However, whether it is for work or not, I am always careful about the way I look because it gives me confidence. I don't spend a lot of time on make-up, make sure that I have the right cosmetics and know how to apply them. I think the time it would take me to look bad is almost the same as it would take me to look good. I mean, as I have to comb my hair anyway, it doesn't take much longer to use a curling tong, or to style it, and as I have to get dressed I might as well make sure that I put on clothes that suit me.

As women, we not only have to know how to juggle family life and work, but we also have to plan ahead and organise. I find this frustrating and sometimes even begrudge Frank for having it so easy.

I remember once when he was going away for three weeks to a cricket event with his mates, I noticed that all he had to do was say, 'Good bye,' without much disruption to his life.

Yet when I am going away, as I often do, I have to sort out clothes for both him and for Christopher, arrange for childcare and school runs between his shifts and days off, organise for my mother to help with the shopping and the meals, and provide a timetable for everyone involved, which includes my sister Carol, who is always willing to help out.

By the time I am ready to leave, far from being like Frank, feeling excited and looking forward to a break or an adventure with the lads, I am tired and stressed and wondering if I have forgotten anything. I resent feeling like this and sometimes see it as a penalty for having a successful career.

This creates tension in my marriage, especially when I make arrangements around Frank and later find that he has changed his shift or has decided to work overtime. Frank is not always helpful when this happens, especially when he suggests that I think about reducing my hours so that I can manage my family commitments better, or give up my job and do something that is more suited to me looking after Christopher.

I wouldn't dream of doing that, not after the time and effort it took for me to get me to get where I am today!

I went to a girls' school where you did well if you went to work in a department store or an office because everything was geared towards you getting married or working in a local packing factory.

I left school with two 'O' levels and office skills, and signed on to an employment agency. I worked as a temp for two years, but after realising that I was unqualified for anything else, I decided on a change of career and went into full-time youth work. I studied for more qualifications at night school, and it was after giving a presentation as part of my course that my tutor suggested I should look at doing some teaching because I had very good communication skills. I took the opportunity and started doing three hours of basic office administration for first-year students. More than satisfied with my input, the head of department increased my hours to six and then nine, and when a job came up for teaching social skills and word-processing, I applied and got it. Leaving my short stint at youth work behind, I worked as a lecturer at the college for six years.

I then started a part-time degree course in marketing and administration. From the outset I knew it was going to take me six years to complete, and while this may seem a long time, I was in no hurry because my salary paid for what I needed, my job gave me practical skills and my studying was a means to improve myself academically and provide me with more opportunities. In this way I was using my time as an investment for my future. Now benefiting from that investment, I was not about to give it up.

If I have to work late, I pay for after-school care so that Christopher can stay on at school until six o'clock. Although I often take work home, I never start anything until I have had some time with Christopher after supper, helping with his homework, reading a book, or watching TV together. Once he is tucked up in bed, only then will I attend to my 'homework.'

I try not to give in to interruptions, but if Christopher is a little restless, because either he's had a bad day at school, or he needs a bit more attention, I will leave my work and see to him. I know that sometimes he is probably manipulating the situation, but he's a child and I have to give him the benefit of the doubt. But not so with Frank when he needs attention, because I expect him to understand when I have to work to deadlines.

He is not always happy about this, but if I set myself a goal I am very disciplined about achieving it. In any case, it does no good to take work home if it only means taking it back undone to the office the next day, and therefore adding it to what I already have to do.

Because I always look presentable, and my nails are long and polished, no matter where I am or what I am doing, some of my friends believe that I don't do housework, but I do. In fact, I like going home and thinking about what I am going to do, where I am going to clean, where I am going to polish and so on. I like to relax in my home and so the environment has to be fresh, clean and inviting. But far from being Superwoman and thinking that I should clean the house from top to bottom, I will prioritise by looking at where needs most cleaning and start there. Sometimes I am able to do all the rooms, other times, if I have had a very busy week, I will only do the sitting room, kitchen and bathroom.

I agree with the importance of having quality time with children and this is a priority for me. Frank's work pattern does not always allow him to spend much time with Christopher, apart from the weekends he has off when he might take Christopher out shopping or play football with him in the garden or the park nearby.

Although Frank and I had been married for about twelve years, it wasn't until I turned thirty-six that I even began to think about having a child. I remember talking it over with my mother, and, although I detected no bitterness in her voice, she warned me that if I wanted to get pregnant I was to get used to the idea of having the child for myself and looking after it, because although Frank would be there, he would not always be there in the way I expected him to be. She was right.

I guess that I have learned how to be assertive with my time, even though it almost lost me a very good friend.

Rosie and I had been friends for years. We shopped together, gossiped together and went to the gym whenever we could, but she was a poor timekeeper and, even though we joked about it, I often felt frustrated at what seemed to be an innate ability to be late.

One morning Rosie asked for a lift into town. I agreed to take her but only if she was on time because I had an important appointment. Although she promised that she would be, she was late and just as I was revving up the car to leave, I could see her hurrying down the road in her usual flustered fashion. Almost breathless, she told me that she had forgotten that it was one of her son's school assemblies and that she had hoped it would be over in time for her to be back and ready.

She then promised to be only a few minutes, but on past history Rosie's few minutes had a habit of turning into ten or even fifteen, and I knew instinctively that if I waited I was going to be late. Accepting that the last thing I wanted to do was create a bad impression to a potential customer, I told Rosie straight that I had to go. As I drove away I could see her standing with arms aloft and mouth wide open in disbelief. I knew she was upset, but it would have been more upsetting for me if I had been late – and I would have had no one to blame but myself.

We met a week later at the gym and, although the atmosphere at first was a little cool, by the end of the session we were talking as normal.

I dropped her home afterwards and as she was about to get out of the car she apologised about that morning and asked if I had made it in time. I had done, with a few minutes to spare.

Even though I have always known the value of time, it really came home to me when my sister Beryl died suddenly a few years ago from a heart defect none of us knew she had. We were all devastated, and it really made me think about how short life really is. Beryl was always saving for something, or thinking about doing this or that, but could never quite make up her mind because of the children, her husband, or some other excuse – and then, of course, it was all too late.

My mother is always saying that time waits for no one, and so on a day-to-day basis I do try to make the most of my time and my life in general. I am not like some people who will just 'make do'. I know what I want and will go full out to get it. I like to surround myself with beautiful things that give me pleasure and if I am going on holiday I will go to places like the Caribbean for the sunshine, the food, and the beauty of the island.

I am often telling my friends, including Rosie, that if there is something they want to do they can always find the time to do it. Right now I am thinking about a new career in the media and so I work as a volunteer with our local community radio to get some experience. It is only for an hour once a week, and although planning the show and finding the people to interview takes time, once again I am developing new skills and taking time to invest in myself.

SUMMARY

Efficient time management is the essence of modern living, in light of increasing pressures through the demanding nature of our jobs and family members. But when family and business are intertwined, even temporary loss of leadership can result in disaster unless time is used with foresight and imagination.

Marie-Henriette's story brings out these points all too clearly. She sets up her own business but from the start she is planning for the future by involving all of her family. No matter how young and how seemingly insignificant their involvement, they learn the best use of time through preparation and good planning.

Managing time means not only managing ourselves but other people. Tasks have to be allocated and work supervised, priorities have to be set and performance measures put in place. But time management also requires the ability to think ahead, as Marie-Henriette does during her period in hospital. A woman of considerable enterprise and determination, despite being physically incapacitated, she uses her time to plan creatively for when she is back in full control of her life.

It is no surprise that, having recovered her health, Marie-Henriette goes on to run a successful chain of restaurants and see her children succeed, in her name, while she now enjoys the pleasures of retirement.

Sylvia's story is rather different, but it does illustrate the importance of scheduling activities and giving priorities to these. Otherwise, we rush from one thing to another and probably never do anything very effectively.

Good time management demands the co-operation and the respect of others. Sylvia's partner has his own career priorities and this often puts domestic burdens onto her. It is a common experience of women in dual-career relationships. But in her generosity to her friend Rosie she also creates problems for herself. She offers to give Rosie a lift into town, but the result is that her own priorities are not respected and acknowledged by her friend. Assertiveness is the name of the game, as well as understanding. Some would wonder why Sylvia needs to spend so much time on her personal appearance, but in her role it is vital if she is to succeed in her career ambitions. For all of us, good time management has to be organised on the basis of priorities and through understanding of others.

Too often people complain of overwork. The cause and the solution to the problem usually rest with the people themselves. It is not unusual for overworked people to find themselves surrounded by others who are not pulling their weight. This is all due to poor time management and the ineffective supervision of others.

SELF-HELP TIPS

- Prioritise activities and schedule the management of time around these.

- Explain your goals and priorities to others so that you gain their respect and support.

- Learn the art of delegation – it saves time and will leave you free to do the things only you can do.

- Managing your own time means managing the time of others. Understand their priorities and negotiate 'Win Win' solutions.

- If you are prone to procrastination, ask yourself why. You should never leave until tomorrow what can be done today. Life is not a rehearsal.

- Working too hard is not a virtue. It is a personal failure of time management.

IN THE CORPORATION

In the uncertain world of the modern corporation, the absence of detailed job descriptions leaves us to organise our own work schedules and prioritise what gets done. Our team leaders expect us to be able to manage ourselves. This means we have to be experts in time management. Otherwise, we suffer from overwork and there is no hope of us ever achieving a satisfactory work–life balance.

In juggling the conflicting work demands that are placed upon us, we have to decide what needs to be done first. We also have to make sure that we concentrate on the things that give us high pay-back. We should always focus on the important issues at the time of day when we are working at our best, and delegate the less important matters to those periods when we know from experience that we are beginning to wind down.

Good time management assumes that we work with others in teams. The effective team leader is the person who is able to distribute tasks to colleagues so that they only focus on the things they are good at. We can only be good time managers if team leadership and other team members allow us to do this.

So many of the experiences of stress and overwork are created by poor time management. We work excessively hard because we fail to delegate to others. We take on too much because of not trusting others to do it.

CHAPTER NINE

MARIANNE AND SUSAN **Controlling Finances**

You often hear people say that money isn't everything, and this may well be true. It is nonetheless one of the most important topics in our lives and one that we should all take time to learn about. But many of us find money difficult to talk about, particularly as it has a way of creating deep resentment and destroying even the best of relationships.

Although some of us may try to save, it is not always easy to be frugal in the face of bombarding images of affluence and apparently 'must have' goods and equipment. The drive to consume invariably leads many of us to spend well above our means as we attempt to keep up with the Joneses – and possibly the Beckhams as well.

But at some time, we are bound to have to ask ourselves whether avoiding our best friend because we can't afford to pay him or her back the money we borrowed, or our dread of the next credit card statement, are worth the swanky designer outfit we splashed out on for that wedding, or the very expensive holiday we took abroad.

As there is an obvious tension between instant gratification and considered frugality, just how should we go about finding the balance?

MARIANNE'S STORY

I was born in Dublin, the first of four children. The Celtic Tiger – the economic boom – was still a good ten years away; indeed, the 1980s are remembered as a time of depression and emigration in Ireland. Luckily, however, both my parents had good jobs and as a child I never wanted for anything, and neither did my younger sister and brothers. By the time I was eight my mother had given up work to stay at home with us. My parents had always planned to have a largish family and so had prudently put away money for the time when my mother decided to give up work. It was only to be for a short period until the youngest of us, my newborn brother, was able to start school.

I had always enjoyed going to school and especially enjoyed learning languages. I soon learned to speak Gaelic Irish, which is compulsory in Irish schools. However, Gaelic wasn't spoken in my home, and the Irish-language TV channel had not yet come into existence and so my experience of Irish was limited to what I learned in school.

My aptitude for languages was proved when I moved up to secondary school and was able to study French, German and Spanish, as well as Irish; I maintained good grades in all four. I took higher-level papers in these subjects, plus English, Maths and History for my Leaving Certificate, the Irish equivalent of A levels, and achieved A grades. I had already sent in my application to the college admissions board and hoped to take a degree course in three languages and also spend my third year studying in a university abroad. The only problem was that the course was not available in Dublin and so I would have to leave home and find accommodation in Cork. The course I hoped to do was pretty intense, without much leeway for me to do a part-time job to help fund myself.

My parents were both adamant that they had always expected me to go to university and had saved enough money for that purpose. If I was willing to make a few sacrifices in regard to clothes, make-up and CDs, all of which I love, they would support me financially. I didn't want to be a burden but throughout my childhood I had seen how prudent my parents were with money and believed them when they said that no one in our family would go short if I went to college in Cork.

In July I received two letters, one informing me of my exam results and another accepting me into University College, Cork. Everybody was excited, especially my seventeen-year-old sister Laura, who seemed to think she would be spending every second weekend or so in my flat away from our parents' watchful eye.

The first semester started in October 2002 and I decided to move down to Cork in September, to get used to my new flatmates and also to being away from home for the first time and living in a new city. Then came the shock. My father suddenly lost his job. It seemed ironic that my parents had always been comfortable during the years of the recession and now, with the so-called boom, they had lost their financial security. I was devastated. How on earth was I going to be able to do this course without my parents' financial support – especially when there were also my sister and brothers to look after?

Not only that, but Laura, who was also very bright, was hoping to study Psychology in two years' time and would be starting university at the same time that I would be studying abroad. My brother, David, would be entering secondary school also in the same year, and I didn't feel that I could possibly ask my parents for any money under these circumstances.

My parents asked me if they could have a couple of days to look at their budget before I went ahead and finalised everything, and I spent those days in my room, crying quietly so they wouldn't know just how upset I was, wondering what I was going to do about my future if I was not able to go to university.

I couldn't believe it when they said that I could still go, although it would not be easy. Since the deposit was paid I would stay in the university accommodation, but after the first semester I would have to find a room off-campus, which would be less expensive but probably a lot less comfortable. To tell the truth, I didn't care if I had to sleep in a cardboard box as long as I could study. They would, of course, be unable to send me as much money as I would need, but I vowed that I would use every penny wisely.

This was only made possible because my mother, who had returned to work on a part-time basis with a large marketing firm, was able to up-grade to a full-time post, whilst my dad took over the housework and looked after my younger brothers and sister.

Reassured over and over again by my parents that everything would be OK, I packed my stuff and arrived in Cork as planned. I really got on with the other girls in my apartment and was a bit upset that I would not be able to stay with them for the full year. However, I soon sorted myself a relatively comfortable room in a house with three other girls who agreed to hold the room for me until January.

On my first day walking around campus I noticed a sign up in the

Students' Centre which read, *Student Staff Required.* When I made enquiries I was told that the shops and cafés around campus had vacancies for students who wanted a job. The pay wasn't as good as what I could earn in a supermarket or shop, or even in a pub – but one thing made me send in an application. Because it was a scheme run by the Students' Union, there would be no pressure on me to put my job before my studies, and they would be understanding when I had exams to sit and essays to hand in; this wouldn't be the case for other businesses, especially around Christmas-time when they would need their staff to work extra hours and I, on the contrary, would need to focus on my college work. Due to the fact that I sent my application in early, there was no difficulty in getting a job in one of the cafés.

My working hours were organised around my class timetable: if I had, say, three hours between lectures I would work in the café for an hour, catch up on assignments for an hour and meet my friends for the last hour. This job proved to be a dream come true for me and I couldn't wait to ring my parents and tell them.

When I got through to my family they had good news for me too. Because my father had been made redundant they had reapplied for a government grant for me and the application had been successful. It wasn't a lot but it was something, and with my new job I started to feel almost rich.

I had regular hours in the café, my parents sent me a cheque every month, and I knew when the three instalments of my government grant were due to be paid. Now was the time to sit down and work out a proper budget. It was a bit scary as all of a sudden I was a grown-up. School was behind me for ever, I had moved out of my parents' house and now I had to work out my own method of financial survival.

My rent in the new house in January would have to be paid monthly so I worked that into my budget from the start. As my parents' cheque would almost cover it, I didn't have to save much money for that. From October I began to put my parents' money away every month, so that when it had to go towards my rent I would be used to not having it there. My wages would have to go towards food and essentials like shampoo; we also had a kitty in the flat to pay for pizza and parties and stuff like that. I had made a lot of friends as well, and didn't want to miss out on trips and other social activities.

I made a list, with food as top priority all the way down to social life at the bottom. It wasn't easy but I knew that I would have to be mature. My parents felt bad that they could not send me as much money as they had calculated, but I knew that if I asked for more they would find it from somewhere. However, I was determined to sacrifice as much as I had to so that I would never need to do that.

I decided that I would do a Big Shop once every three weeks, when I would go to the cheap foreign supermarket and stock up on pasta, jam, sugar, sauces and beans which were half the price. My meat I got at the English market every week; the prices were good and the portions were much bigger. Things like milk and bread were bought out of the kitty so I put money aside for that.

Other things that I needed were biros and notepads and folders. I used my parents' first cheque to stock up during the back-to-school sales in the stationery shops around the city. Things like shampoo I bought once every three weeks during my Big Shop. I found that a lot of chemists had offers like 'three for the price of two' every month or so, and always tried to time my Big Shop for when there was one of these promotions on somewhere. If there wasn't I would simply do my food Big Shop one week and my essentials Big Shop the next. My friends soon started to laugh and ask when was my next Big

Shop coming up, but having little headings for everything helped me to keep things organised.

I was very strict with myself about how much I would use my mobile phone. At first I would send text messages to everyone, just to say hello, but soon found how much my credit was being used up. After that, I only sent important messages, like where to meet someone, and then when we were face to face, we would have our conversation. It worked out much cheaper!

With some real imaginative budgeting, I was still left with money to go out with when all the important things were covered. But my planning didn't end there. Many places had college nights during the week and so it was cheaper to go out then than at weekends. Companies did promotions around campus and gave tickets for free drinks, clubs often handed out vouchers for free admission or a concession on the price, things like that. So I always made sure that wherever I was planning to go, there was some sort of deal. None of my friends had much money either and so there was always someone I could persuade to come with me.

I did still allow myself the odd treat every now and then. After my Big Shop was done and I had everything I needed, I went shopping for clothes and the odd accessory. I tried to look for bargains most of the time but I also splashed out every now and then on a pair of jeans or a nice top.

Because everyone had exams at different times there was always someone who needed time off work. If I had a quiet week, with no assignments or tests, I would do an extra couple of hours in the café. I didn't spend as much money as my friends either, because as I worked between lectures I didn't sit around eating buns and drinking coffee like they did. By the end of the year, I was almost the only one in the house who was not broke and sending begging messages home to my parents.

I am halfway through my second year now, and am well used to managing my money. I never consciously noticed it, but my parents' sensible attitude to money probably influenced me while I was growing up.

During the summer I got a job in a shop during the day and did three hours' cleaning three nights a week. Everyone praised me for my discipline but I hate to admit it was only so I could go out as much as I want this year and splash out a bit more often. It also feels good when I can tell my parents they don't need to send me as much money this month, or when I can give my brothers and sister some pocket-money.

I have also managed to start putting money away for my year abroad. I am grateful to my parents for not only supporting me but teaching me how to manage my money.

SUSAN'S STORY

I was the middle daughter of five children living on an estate in Liverpool, and I often felt as if I was the forgotten one, because whilst my parents used to make a fuss over my brothers and sisters, they would often say that I was intelligent and smart enough for them not to have to worry about me.

This led me to become a bit of a loner at home, spending hours in my room reading, playing with my toys or just dreaming. But I was good at school and enjoyed being in the classroom situation. The teachers knew that I was bright, and the highlight of my school year was our final exams, when I looked forward to showing how well I could do.

I wanted to train to be a teacher, but instead of going to college I had to find a job because my income was required to help support our family.

Like most of the families in our neighbourhood we didn't have a lot and I was amazed at how hard both my parents, and particularly my mother, had to work to make sure that we had all that we needed.

I can remember Friday evenings when my father used to hand over money to my mother. I never knew how much it was, only that it was never enough, and the fact that he would then spend most of the weekend drinking with friends explained why.

I got a job on a youth training scheme and earned £23 a week. I gave half of this to my parents, for my keep and food, gave some pocket-money to my younger brother and sister, and kept a little for myself. I calculated exactly how much I needed to survive and even had a bit left over which I would put away.

At the end of the scheme I found myself out of work again, and unable to find a job I signed on for unemployment benefit. At this time, and with all of us still living at home, including my two older sisters, we were more than a little tight for space. By then I was eighteen and, deciding that I was well able to look after myself, I left home and found myself a one-bedroom council flat.

It was my first taste of independence and I was excited, until I realised that, although I had managed to save a little money, it was nowhere near the amount I needed to furnish the property. There was a store I knew that advertised hire purchase: a customer could choose the goods they wanted and then agree to pay a certain amount, on a weekly or monthly basis.

The whole process was quite simple – a few questions, my signature on the agreement form and within thirty minutes arrangements were being made for the delivery of a bed, a table and four chairs, and a settee to my flat.

Managing to pick up a few things from my parents, buying other bits and pieces second-hand, and making all the curtains myself, within a few months my little flat began to feel like home.

I never stopped looking for a job and later found one as a cleaner. The pay wasn't brilliant, but I was able to get by. Then I fell pregnant with my first child, Kevin, and although my job would be kept open for me, I knew that I had to keep a close eye on my finances.

Deciding to start with my hire purchase, I called into the store to check on my outstanding balance. I had been paying for nearly three years and was astonished to see that after all this time the balance remained the same! When I mentioned this to the manager he said that I was paying the interest and it would be another year or so before I started to reduce the amount of money I had borrowed. I couldn't believe what I was hearing and when he repeated it, I simply said that I wasn't prepared to pay any more money if the balance was going to stay the same. He then said that I had to, otherwise the company would take me to court. I told him to go ahead and take me to court, and then walked out of the store.

Sure enough, I found myself in court a few months later and a set payment was arranged for me to pay each month. It was OK, because during the time the case took to get to court, I was saving what I would have had to pay anyway. The amount that was agreed was well within what I could afford, and at least I didn't have to wait another year to see any reduction. What I didn't know was that this would make it difficult for me to get any other credit, but in a way that didn't matter, because after that experience I wasn't about to get myself in debt again.

But worse was yet to come when I moved from my one-bedroom council flat to a two-bedroom one.

For weeks I had been going back and forth to the Housing Department asking about the new rent I had to pay, and each time I was told that it was being assessed. This dragged on for months, until two years later, I was presented with rent arrears of £2,000. Having argued my point about my case not having been dealt with earlier, I was able to negotiate an agreed amount that I could comfortably pay every month.

It took me eleven years to clear my debt, by which time I had another two children, Krystal and Jonathon.

Although my children's father, Adam, was often around, we never lived together because, whilst I had a steady job, working in a canteen, he was in and out of work and I couldn't rely on him financially. Times were hard, and my first obligation was to my children and to make sure that their needs were met. Living with Adam would have interrupted my plans because I would not only have to share myself again but I would have less control over my finances. Although I loved him, I didn't relish the thought of Adam being able to influence the way I was spending my money or to be making financial demands on me. I had seen how much pressure some of my friends were under to make ends meet when they were the main breadwinners, and more often than not it was the children who suffered. I wasn't about to let that happen to my children or me.

Money is important to keep relationships going, especially if you want to do things together. But putting my children first meant that my leisure activities had to be limited, because I just didn't have the spare cash and didn't want to live above my means.

Having to keep to a tight budget, I would ask the children what they wanted to eat and then organise a menu for the week. During my weekly shopping I would incorporate everything I needed for the menu and, by doing so, make sure that I was only buying what was required. If a tin of beans or something else that I would normally buy was left over, it was taken off the following week's shopping list and this would be a saving. It might only have been thirty pence or so, but in my situation every penny had to count and it's amazing how it can build up.

I was once able to save up to £1,500 over a period of time, simply because I saw money that I didn't use, or was left over, as money that I didn't need and would put away. Although that sum was my rainy day money, I never actually had to use any of it until some went towards buying my first car.

Every two weeks I would buy clothes for the children, which could range from a large item, such as a dress or coat, to something smaller like panties or socks. When I was growing up, I was very aware of my sisters and brother getting more things than I did, and I didn't think that was fair. I wanted to make sure that my children were treated equally and so I would put by up to £20 a week for each child so that they all had something every month.

When it came to buying appliances, I would set my price range but I would never buy something without first reading the brochure. If I found that an appliance was more efficient and would last much longer but cost more than what my budget would allow, then I was prepared to pay what I would set as an upper limit of about another £50.

Whenever I did this, I would juggle what I was spending on food, or leave something that was not urgent until I had recouped the extra money I had paid out on the appliance. By doing this, I always managed to stay within my overall budget.

But I also had to guard against the hard sell around getting extra insurance cover. If I was going to pay £200 for extra insurance cover over a five-year period on a machine that might or might not go wrong, or was only made to last between two or three years, I knew I was better off saving my money to buy a new machine, especially as technology is improving all the time.

When I am budgeting I have to see the whole picture.

For instance, when I was looking to change my washing machine, I saw one with a massive drum. This would not only be more economical, but would make my life easier by enabling me to wash more clothes in one cycle. But having measured the dimension of the space I had in my kitchen, I found I would have to pay for some reconstruction work so that the machine could fit in. I didn't bother, because although I could afford to buy the machine I could not afford to pay for the additional work to accommodate it.

I find it easier to budget on a weekly basis because I can see what I have for that week, am able to manage it effectively, and whatever is left I can carry over to the next week or save. On a monthly basis it is not so easy to juggle because I may not always see when the opportunity presents itself for me to make savings. Psychologically it is also easier for me to accept putting away £5 a week than to pay out £20 a month!

I don't have credit cards because I don't want to get into debt and have to pay interest. There has been the odd occasion when I have seen something and I knew I could buy it on credit if I had a card, but I discipline myself and say that it is better for me to save and to get it later.

Whenever I give my children pocket-money, whilst I don't tell them how to spend it I always encourage them to save a little because it is never too early to teach children the value of money and the need to be prudent.

If I haven't got something I won't put myself in debt to get it. Life is stressful enough and I see little point in taking on more problems like having to worry about how to manage to pay this creditor without another one being on your back.

But not all credit is bad and if I were ever to consider using credit again I would look for a store that offered something like six months interest-free. Although the interest is likely to be already incorporated in the publicised price, at least you can see at first hand how much you have to pay.

With the children getting older and needing more, I have two jobs and continue to work around them. I have never been one to frown on doing a particular job as long as it paid me enough to keep my home and family. I've worked in a clothes factory, worked as commercial cleaner, as a nursing assistant in an old people's home, in a canteen and in a shoe shop. At one time I was even self-employed as a partner in a cosmetics business.

I still live on a council estate, and very often when I come home from work all kinds of literature has come through the letter-box promoting cash and credit. I remember being offered £2,000 to buy furniture purely on the basis of two forms of ID, such as a household bill, a benefits book or a driver's licence. I binned this offer straight away but I know that many people – particularly if they are unemployed – are vulnerable to these offers and get sucked into borrowing because they need ready cash. It's only later, when they realise they may have to pay up to 50 per cent interest on what they have borrowed, that they find themselves in deep trouble.

I remember seeing how my parents had to struggle so that we didn't miss out on anything, and thinking how awful it would be not to have money. I can't imagine what it would be like being in a situation like that and, believe me, I never want to find out.

SUMMARY

Both these stories illustrate the importance of financial control. They show how crucial it is not to be 'conned' by the offer of 'free' credit and hire-purchase agreements. Each of the women is aware of their vulnerability to be ripped off because of their insecure financial circumstances.

For Marianne and Susan, planning is central to their financial management skills. They look ahead in terms of their personal needs and organise their spending patterns around these.

In their different ways, neither sees herself as a victim of economic hardship. They recognise that they have financial obligations, and for these money has to be earned. To this end, they are flexible about the jobs they are prepared to do. They will literally do anything to earn enough money to make ends meet. More than this, they are able to put money aside for a rainy day, for the emergencies and contingencies that are likely to crop up.

Susan's story is typical of the hundreds of thousands of lone parents. She is dedicated to the economic and emotional well-being of her children, and through her financial planning has developed sophisticated skills in money management. She has become a very skilful negotiator, a discriminating shopper and an acute financial planner. She recognises the downside of debt and the traps that people fall into through offers of 'zero' interest rates and dubious insurance policies. Through all of this, she gains an emotional and psychological independence that many women would love to have. Who needs men?

Marianne is a young student. Her parents are able to provide for her, but she chooses to be self-sufficient. She operates within a tight budget set by what she is able to earn. This means she is able to regard her parents' contributions as a bonus. Like Susan, Marianne is very price-sensitive. She knows exactly where to buy goods, at what time and at what price. She is an entrepreneur in the making.

SELF-HELP TIPS

- Never rely on credit and hire-purchase agreements. They are a 'rip-off' and add to economic hardship.

- Learn how to go without or, for essential goods, buy second-hand instead of on credit.

- Outgoings should never be greater than incomings. This means that planning, 'looking ahead' and 'saving for a rainy day' are essential features of sound financial management.

- Exercise strict self-discipline and always purchase within budget.

- Be a good negotiator because there are always bargains to be had and discounts on offer. If you don't ask, you don't get.

IN THE CORPORATION

All organisations have finance directors and others respon-sible for controlling the economic survival of the business. But we live in a world of devolved budgets. In most organisations, budgets are devolved to operational units such as depart-ments, sections and functional teams.

It means that all of us are now responsible for managing budgets and ensuring that we do not overspend. Cashflows have to be managed and income and expenditure accounts carefully monitored. We are often held personally responsible for any overspends that occur as a result of decisions we take within our own operational units.

Many of us are afraid of money. We stick our heads in the sand. We will turn down the offer of promotion simply because it will require financial responsibilities, and yet we are quite happy to prudently manage our personal financial affairs. Are corporate budgets so different from household income and expenditure skills?

Whatever our key skills in whatever sphere of any organisa-tion, we also have to be capable of managing and understand-ing corporate business. It is essential for survival on the road to the corporate boardroom.

CHAPTER TEN

AYO AND JULIE **Pursuing Strategies**

If you are one of those carefree people who always seem to fall on your feet, you indeed have luck on your side – because with the complexity of life today, it is hard to see how any of us can achieve anything of substance without making plans.

It may be of course that we are simply happy enough to get by, accepting whatever comes our way, and convincing ourselves that we are making the most of life. Or if there is a deeper yearning for something else, we deny what we are feeling because we are not exactly sure what it is.

As it is hard to be 'exactly sure' about anything, we have to be prepared to try new things, to take risks and seize new opportunities. Whether it is an obligation or a particular goal we are setting ourselves, we are more likely to succeed if we take time to think, plan and act on our decisions.

However, mindful of the fact that there is always the possibility of things not working out the way we want them to, what would you do in such circumstances? Berate yourself for having failed, or take stock and try again?

AYO'S STORY

I grew up in a reasonably well-off Nigerian family. My father was a barrister and although my mother worked full-time as a civil servant she was able to balance this with running the home and raising a family. My parents travelled a lot and I was born the second of four girls in London, where they were studying at the time. Although I felt 100 per cent African, London was always going to be a very special place for me.

In a house full of books and with a father who seemed to know everything, it was easy to learn, and without a great deal of effort I became very successful at school, took my A levels two years early and by seventeen years old was studying for a degree in Economics.

My father was my role model and I picked up a lot of his habits. When he came home from work he was forever making notes about who he had met that day and storing information about them for 'future reference' he would say – so I did the same. He was an inspiration, and we were all encouraged to be ambitious and successful in whatever we wanted to do.

At the age of twenty and after gaining my degree in Economics, I signed up for my National Service, as both male and female graduates in Nigeria were expected to do. I was posted to a college in a small coastal town where I provided counselling and guidance in careers for young people between the ages of twelve and eighteen.

We also had to do some military training and it was during this time that I met my husband, Olu, who was an officer in the army and had come to oversee the training we were doing.

The drilling and assault course were tough, and by the time we finished I was looking forward to relaxing in the evening with friends at one of the many parties and social events that took place on the campus.

I was sitting on my own in the main hall, waiting for friends to join me, when Olu came over. He was very pleasant, and after a lengthy conversation we found out that we had a lot in common, particularly around family friends and things that we were both interested in.

We saw each other a few more times before he left the college, and got engaged when my National Service was over. Three years later we were married.

Although my parents were reasonably happy about my marriage, looking back I can see that my father was afraid that I would abandon my education. But Olu's position in the army meant that he was often posted abroad for long periods of time, and so, deciding to use the time that we were apart to build up my career, I started another degree in Accountancy.

Eighteen months into my degree I became pregnant but continued with my coursework until our son, Ife, was born.

My mother offered to look after Ife so that I could complete my training, but Olu had other plans and one day announced, quite out of the blue, that he wanted us to emigrate to England. A few of our friends and families had already settled there and he wanted us to join them.

My parents, who were unhappy about the situation, suggested that we should wait a while, at least until I had finished my studies, but Olu was impatient. He wanted us to leave as soon as possible since he feared that any delay might give my parents time to talk us out of going.

I, too, had reservations, but the chance to return to London was so tempting – and in any case Olu was adamant that we should go and, as his wife, my place was by his side.

In preparation I started to write to friends in London asking for details and information about rented accommodation. Although Olu suggested that we could stay with friends, I had no intention of doing so because I knew of people who had outstayed their welcome and been told to leave by families and friends who had agreed to put them up when they first arrived in England.

Months later, I arrived in London with Ife, and within a week we had moved into temporary accommodation, while Olu worked out his six months' notice with the army. It was a daunting prospect for me, having to live alone with our baby son in an environment I was not used to, but it worked out well because I had time to find my way around and to look after Ife.

I missed Olu but, knowing that he would be joining us within a few months, I didn't mind the short time I had to wait, and even the cold nights and the lonely existence were not too bad as I could study and write about all the new things that I was experiencing.

I also wrote a letter to myself in which I detailed how I wanted my life to be – I wanted another child, I wanted a good education for my children, I wanted to be self-sufficient, and to be well-paid and respected for my work. When I finished the letter I sealed it in an envelope and placed it in a box with other papers and cards.

By the time Olu arrived, Ife was in pre-nursery school, we had moved into a council house and I had found a job. But Olu didn't find it as easy to settle because he was a black man in a white country and anything but diplomatic. Used to being upfront in the army and commanding his men, he thought that his usual abrupt and authoritative approach would work as well here, but it didn't, and even though I tried to help him adopt a more moderate approach he was reluctant to change.

In the months before he joined me, I had kept a journal of discriminating and prejudicial experiences I had heard about, like a black woman who had an English name and was told to come into an office for a job interview, only to find when she got there that the vacancy had suddenly gone.

I felt that if employers got past Olu's name, which in itself was likely to be a barrier, he had to present himself in a more positive way, no matter what he was feeling, if he was to stand any chance of getting the job. After talking this over with him, he changed his approach and managed to secure a number of jobs before being accepted into the regular army.

Olu's contract with the army was only for a year and, pregnant with our second child, I advised him to think about what he was going to do after that. But rather than plan ahead, he simply said he was sure that things would fall into place.

I was frustrated by this, because I had responsibilities and ambitions for our children and so needed to have firm plans and back-up positions, even on simple matters like having a main babysitter but also a few others that I could call upon if I needed to.

For the next few years, Olu moved in and out of work, and as he was often employed only for a few months, and once for almost a year, life became very hard. Most of my friends, who were professionals and would come on holiday to London with their children, were surprised to see how we had to struggle. They implored us to come home, saying that they could find us both good jobs.

I felt myself being pulled from one direction to another, thinking about resuming a life back home in Nigeria that I knew would be more enriching, and yet feeling the need to stay with my husband and not to disrupt the education of our children. I discussed this situation with Olu, and he was adamant that we should stay.

For a number of years we carried on with Olu's irregular work pattern and me raising and organising the family, working full-time and taking a business management course to increase my chances of promotion. Then one cold dark night walking home during a Tube strike I remember saying to myself that this had got to stop: I was not happy, our marriage was not working and my children were in an atmosphere full of tension.

As the months rolled by I was simply going through the motions of being a wife, looking after the children and the house, going to work, coming home and cooking the meals. Then one morning, realising that I had had enough, I decided that I would leave Olu.

He was out of work again at this time and I felt that I should wait until he found another job and could look after himself before leaving. His family were already blaming me for not supporting him enough in finding work, and it would simply add to their resentment if I left him when he was unemployed.

But then Olu suddenly and without any discussions decided to go to law school back in Nigeria: by the time he told me, his flight was already booked and he was due to leave in two weeks.

I was stunned at first but also relieved because it gave me the opportunity to tell him about how I was feeling, especially when he asked if I would still be there for him when he returned. When I said that I could not guarantee it, he simply packed his things and left.

After he had gone I took the day off work and sat and planned how life was going to be. That night I talked with Ife and his brother, Tunde, and explained to them that their father had left, and, as we would have to look after ourselves now, life was going to be very different from what they had been used to.

I then went to my study to begin writing letters to people who needed to be told about the changes that we were compelled to make.

My first priority was to think about where we were going to live. With Olu gone I calculated that most of my money would be spent on paying the rent on our three-bedroomed semi-detached council house, and that I would not be able to afford the deposit to buy our own house. Also, the house held too many bad memories for me, and all I wanted to do was to leave so that I could begin my life again with my children. My first letter, therefore, was to the Housing Department of the Borough Council.

I then wrote to my university, requesting time out from my course so that I could deal with everything that needed to be done without the added pressure of having to study.

I also wrote to my children's school so that, if there were any problems with the boys on account of the break-up, the teachers would understand why. Money was going to be very tight, and so I budgeted down to the last penny and told the boys that we had to manage on much less than we had before.

When I spoke with my employers about my situation, they were very supportive and accepted my request for flexible time, which would allow me to work around the school-run, which Olu had looked after during his periods between jobs, and also to do more work from home.

Within two weeks of Olu leaving, I had put all my large pieces of furniture into storage and we were looking for somewhere else to live.

Having researched the situation regarding purchasing a house I discovered a scheme whereby we could move into a council-run hostel, which didn't sound very attractive but had one big advantage – if we lived there for one or two years, the monthly rent of £800 would be deducted from the price of any house that I wanted to purchase. The rent was a littler higher than we could afford, but, as it was a means of helping me to be in a better position eventually to buy a property, we signed on to the scheme.

Within weeks we had moved into the hostel and were living in one room – my eleven- and eight-year-old sons and me. We had our own bathroom but had to share everything else with another twelve people. It was hard going, but I knew it was worth making sacrifices in the short term if I wanted to build a secure future for the children and myself. My father had always taught me that to gain something in life often meant having to sacrifice other things on the way.

I believed this, but at times I wondered whether I was in fact sacrificing too much, especially at night when the lights had to go out at around eight o'clock so that the boys could get some sleep.

Once they had settled, I would go across the corridor to my neighbour, Julie, either to continue with work I had to do, or just to sit, sometimes in tears, thinking about whether I was doing the right thing. It was at these times that I often wondered what my father would have done, and believing that it might have been something similar gave me the strength to continue.

We heard nothing from Olu until he turned up at the hostel six months later. Things had not worked out for him and he had come to see if we could try again to be a family. But I had moved on and had no intention of going back. It was up to him to rebuild his relationship with his sons and I offered to help support him in doing that for their sake.

After spending almost a year in the hostel, I found a three-bedroom townhouse, and taking advantage of the scheme was able to buy the house and begin to reorganise our lives.

As I unpacked a few boxes I found the letter I had written to myself long before the break-up of my marriage. It was addressed to 'Darling Ayo' and outlined the goals that I had set for myself years before. I was proud that I had managed to achieve most of them.

Both my sons are happy and doing well at school, and I have almost completed my degree course. I am looking forward to the rest of my life, going full steam ahead and making every effort to achieve the new personal goals I have set out for myself.

JULIE'S STORY

I was fortunate enough to be part of a good circle of friends that had built up over the years. A core of us had known each other from school or university whilst other people drifted in and out as partners or colleagues from work.

That's how I met Geoff. He was a civil engineer who had moved to Birmingham from London and worked with Stephen, whom I had known for about ten years. Wanting to help him settle in, Stephen invited Geoff to a bowling session we had organised one Saturday evening.

Geoff was a striking and handsome figure with short dark hair and the most amazing deep blue eyes I had ever seen. Stephen introduced him to everyone and, as usual with newcomers, we all did what we could to make him feel at ease.

When the bowling session was over, a few of us, including Geoff, went on to a Balti restaurant and I found myself sitting next to him and browsing through the menu with him. Stephen's impish smile made me wonder whether or not I was being set up.

Our group was a mixture of couples and singles. Thirty-five and single myself, I wasn't particularly looking for a relationship, but neither was I averse to having one should the right man come along. It was far too soon to know whether that man was Geoff, but we got on well and I wouldn't have minded seeing him again.

At the end of the evening we all went our separate ways, and although we did not know when we were likely to meet up again as a large group, we would certainly be seeing each other as individuals or would be staying in touch by phone.

One evening, Stephen called. He asked how I was and we made small talk about work and life in general. Then, and quite out of the blue, he asked me what I thought of Geoff. I was taken aback at first, but said that I thought he was OK. Stephen then said Geoff had asked for my number but he didn't feel that it was right to let him have it without my approval.

More than a little excited, I told Stephen that it was fine for Geoff to have my number, and when he phoned a few days later we started seeing each other.

We were enraptured and totally inseparable for the first few months. I had never been happier, and things were destined to get better when Geoff moved out of his studio flat and we started living together in my three-bedroomed townhouse. After a number of failed relationships, I had forgotten how wonderful it was to be intimate with someone again, and most of my friends said how good we looked together.

Being with Geoff had also tempered my biological clock, which was ticking louder than usual as I approached my thirty-sixth year!

The next time we all met up as a group was when Sara, one of our long-time friends, returned from Australia where she had been work-ing for a year. She looked well and spoke vivaciously about her experiences. Later in the evening she asked after Geoff and, when I told her that we were an item, she congratulated me on what she described as a 'good catch'.

We were eighteen months into our relationship when I felt that something was going wrong.

Geoff had started to become a little distant and unresponsive, and when asked blamed it on his work. Knowing that the firm had cap-tured a major contract, I wasn't concerned about the number of times he had to work late or the weekends he said he had to spend on site.

But I had cause for concern about what was happening to us. We hardly went out together any more and when we did, for a meal, or to the pictures, he showed little enthusiasm for either. I was further disappointed when he said that he found some of my friends tiresome and no longer wanted to socialise with them, or the group. But worse than that, we hardly made love any more, and when we did it was without the passion I had been used to.

Although I had always been a self-assured and motivated person, I began to feel depressed and I knew it was bad when colleagues commented on how lacklustre I had become.

Then one evening, Geoff appeared distressed and said that we had to talk. When I asked what was wrong, he simply said that he had met someone else and thought it only fair to tell me. He then added that he would be moving his things out that weekend.

I was devastated. Confused, too. I couldn't think how this could possibly have happened when we had been so close. Unable to make any sense of the situation, I became very angry and demanded answers as to who this person was and how long he had been seeing her.

We argued but Geoff refused to say who it was; it didn't matter anyway, he said, because his mind was made up and he was leaving. He then packed a few things, said he would be back for the rest, and left.

The house was suddenly emptier than it had ever been before and I was a crumpled heap on the floor.

In the days that followed, I learned that the other woman was Sara and that Geoff and she had started seeing each other after the

Christmas party we had all been to at her house. I was livid and terribly hurt by a sense of betrayal, not only by Geoff but by everyone else in the group, including Stephen.

For weeks I wandered around in a daze and couldn't focus on my work or myself, and when the pain was too much to bear I took some time off sick. Sinking deeper into dark depression, I tormented myself for having been such a fool, for failing to see what was going on. I shuddered at the thought of how people must have been laughing behind my back.

At night I found it hard to sleep, and in the morning saw little point in getting out of bed. I lived on cream crackers because I couldn't be bothered to cook and moved in slovenly fashion around the house in an old dressing-gown, because I couldn't be bothered to get dressed.

None of my previous relationships had ended like this. Admittedly there had been tears, but on the whole there were good reasons for separation and the few short flings I had embarked upon were fun and without commitment. But this was different. I had loved and trusted Geoff, and there was nothing to suggest that we could not have had a good future together.

I cried a lot, and it was during one of these outbursts that I caught sight of myself in the mirror: I saw the dishevelled hair, black-rimmed eyes through lack of sleep, and a face that was drawn and much older than my years.

The man I loved had left me and because of that I was punishing myself and on the verge of wrecking my whole life.

How or when I had come to this was beyond me, but the shock of seeing how I looked stirred something inside me, and I knew instinctively that I had to find ways back to being the lively, self-assured and independent person that I had been before.

One sure way of doing that was to get back to doing all the things I had given up when Geoff and I got together. Things like my mid-week sessions at the gym, evenings and weekends out with the girls, my sports and the walks I used to go on with friends. It was time I paid some attention to me.

I looked around at my untidy house and decided to start there. But it wasn't just about cleaning and putting things neatly in their place. I began throwing out things that I had hoarded for years. I then returned the furniture to where it had been before Geoff moved in and retrieved things from the attic that I loved having around me. I dusted and polished and bought fresh flowers, which I arranged in the hallway, the living room and the kitchen. In no time at all my little house, which had become a dark prison, was transformed into a bright and sweet-smelling haven.

I lit candles and placed them in the bathroom and took a long and soothing bubble bath. During this time I allowed myself to replay the good times that Geoff and I had had. I cried a little, too, but it wasn't with the anger and resentment of before, but with an acceptance of the sadness and the loss of someone I had loved with every inch of my being.

For the first time in weeks I was able to sleep, and when morning came I was able to get out of bed because I had a life to live.

I did not expect that everything would be back to normal immediately because I was still hurting inside and had no idea when it would stop. But being able to tend to matters on the outside, I decided on a haircut. My dark brown hair had been shoulder-length when I met Geoff, but because he liked long hair I had allowed it to grow. I could see from glossy magazines that short and sexy styles were in and I wanted one of them. But I went even further than that and had a complete beauty treatment.

I started back at the gym and caught up with some of the girls I hadn't seen for months. I didn't realise how out of shape I was, something a few of them said must have been down to good living, and if I was honest it certainly had been.

Back at work I felt energised and knew I had done the right thing when people commented on my new and rather 'chic' look. I also knew that I had almost arrived when someone said it was good to have me back!

For the first few weeks I felt great, and then without warning I found myself wilting again. Even though I had done well on my own, I suddenly realised that my recovery would not be complete without my friends, and Stephen in particular.

I was angry with everyone when Geoff left, and so had cut myself off from the group, thinking that I would never trust any one of them again. It was now time to swallow my pride and so I picked up the phone to call Stephen. It was Jackie, Stephen's partner, who answered the phone. She asked how I was getting on. Not wanting to prolong the conversation as it was Stephen I wished to speak to, I told her that I was fine and asked if she would get Stephen to call me when he came home. She promised that she would. For the rest of the evening I waited for that call, wanting desperately to apologise and to know when we could meet.

I was about to go to bed at around eleven o'clock when the phone rang. I wept as I heard Stephen's voice. I told him how sorry I was for what I had said when I accused him of siding with Geoff and Sara against me and for not being the friend I thought that he was. He was great and said he understood and probably would have acted in the same way.

He then told me that he had found out about Sara and Geoff only a week before Geoff confessed to me, and it was he who had told him to come clean with me otherwise he, Stephen, would have told me. No one else knew what was going on because they had not seen Geoff and Sara together, but once they found out a few people were upset that it had happened.

I broke down again, remembering what I had said to people and wondering how I could have been so wrong. But Stephen was sure they would understand and, if I wanted to, we could go for a drink or I could come over.

I took up Stephen's invitation. We met for a drink, and were later joined by a few others. There were kisses and hugs all around and I was grateful for their support. They said I didn't deserve what had happened, but on reflection no one could really say how else it should have happened.

It isn't a crime for someone's partner to fall in love with another person; it is happening all the time. Geoff and I had fallen for each other and what we had was good, until Sara came along and he was more attracted to her than to me. It was obvious that she could give him something I was not capable of giving. No matter how he left me, I was still going to get hurt.

I was growing in strength until one day when I was rummaging through some papers I found a photograph of Geoff and me when we were on holiday in Italy. I had to admit that I was still grieving in a way, but at least the pain was much less than it had been before.

I recognised that I was always going to have memories of our relationship, some good and some bad, and knew also that the things I loved about Geoff would probably stay with me for a long time. But what about the things I *didn't* like about him?

The way he left the toilet seat up after using it, and left the cap off the toothpaste, the odd smelly sock abandoned under the bed, the way he picked his nose and wiped his hands across his lips, how he snored and grunted in his sleep, the way he passed wind first thing in the morning and how he belched after eating.

As a therapeutic exercise I decided to write down the things I had disliked about Geoff, and after filling two sides of paper felt sure that they would serve as a reminder of what I no longer had to put up with because of the love I had for him.

Within days, the last memories of Geoff had been consigned to the bin and it was when I started to feel a little sorry for Sara that I realised I was well and truly back to my old self and to the person I needed to love and look after most. Me.

SUMMARY

These two stories show the importance of planning ahead, the need to develop personal strategies if short-term crises are to be overcome. To put it another way, events do not dictate our lives. It is our lives that dictate events.

Ayo and Julie could so easily regard themselves as victims and do nothing to improve their lot. Instead they take stock of themselves and, on the basis of this, develop long-term strategies for moving on. Julie is devastated by the break-up of her relationship with her partner. She feels bitterly let down and conned by her friends. Her self-confidence is utterly destroyed and she moves into a period of deep depression. She allows her personal appearance to deteriorate, her house to become untidy. In general terms, her life is in free-fall. Until she looks at herself in the mirror.

This is a crucial moment for her. She realises the emotional, psychological and physical depths to which she has sunk. She suddenly recognises the need to develop a personal strategy for survival. She has to give up the past and move on. In this, she assesses her own personal strengths and weaknesses. She also lists the strengths and weaknesses of her ex-partner. She comes to the conclusion that his weaknesses are far greater than his strengths. She no longer has to put up with his farting, belching and picking his nose.

This releases her from the emotional grip of her previous relationship so she can start a new life. The next task for her is to implement a strategy to do this. She re-establishes contact with her friends, goes to the gym to get fit and has a 'makeover' to present herself to others as a 'new person'. Through this, she regains her self-respect and, more importantly, discovers her true self.

Ayo's experience is acted out a thousand times every day in modern Britain. Here is a woman, married and with a family, but then suddenly things fall apart. Her relationship with her husband deteriorates so they split up. Ayo finds she has to develop a strategy for economic survival. In this sense, her circumstances are different to those of Julie. Ayo has children to feed and must ensure there is a roof over their heads.

But Ayo is not a victim. She could so easily have relied on state handouts. Instead, she creates a strategy for herself and her children which she successfully implements over a couple of years. So much so, in fact, that when her husband returns, wanting to re-start the relationship, she is so self-confident and independent that she rejects his proposals.

SELF-HELP TIPS

- Never make panic reactions to crises. They can only be resolved through careful, rational planning. They demand the working out and execution of well-thought-through strategies.

- Be prepared to acquire and develop the personal skills required to achieve the newly stated strategic goals.

- Personal strategies are about looking forward, not reflecting back. Practical thinking comes from the future, not the past.

- Consider your personal strengths and weaknesses. How can you build on the first and compensate for the latter?

IN THE CORPORATION

In the corporation of the past, there was a clear separation between strategic and operational responsibilities. There were those whose prime duty was to plan ahead, to forecast and to map out the future direction of the company. For others, it was to execute and to implement those strategies through various operational processes.

Today, this distinction is no longer possible. The more dynamic and ever-changing business environment requires everyone in the organisation to be able to respond to change in very flexible ways. They have to anticipate likely problems and work out possible solutions. It means that we all have to think and act strategically. Emergent problems do not offer their own solutions. Only we can offer the solutions but usually only by being ahead of the game.

Some people are able to think more strategically than others. And it is those who have had more turbulent life experiences who are better equipped to come up with strategic solutions. These experiences have forced them to be adaptive, flexible and always to try to be ahead of the game. They have developed creative and imaginative ways of thinking which affect their attitudes towards problem-solving.

It is these people who are likely to get to the boardroom table. Their more varied and challenging life experiences make them well suited to cope with the ever-changing, complex problems that are thrown up in the everyday circumstances of the modern corporation.

CHAPTER ELEVEN

CLAUDETTE AND RHIANA **Managing Change**

Have you ever had a defining moment in your life? A near-accident, the loss of a friend or a loved one, the break-up of a relationship, having to leave a job you have done for years, or something as simple as watching a television programme or reading an article in a newspaper?

Whatever the moment, the impact might lead to a short-term reaction, or to a longer-term commitment to change. That change, however, isn't always easy, especially if it means breaking lifetime habits or transforming attitudes and behaviour.

Taking that first step is sometimes daunting, and as you continue there will be times when you falter, begin to question your own judgement and, especially if you are on your own, feel like giving up.

Some women we have spoken to say that this is the time when they need to find a little extra courage and determination to stick to what they have decided to do. Others say that the thought of how pleased so-called friends, and sometimes family members, would be if they failed is enough to keep them going.

Just how difficult is it to overcome barriers to transforming yourself into the person you have always known that you could be?

CLAUDETTE'S STORY

It was seventeen years after I had seen what I wanted to become before I actually achieved it.

The youngest of five girls, born to Jamaican parents, I was spoilt by almost everyone. With long hair that was neatly plaited in two and tied with ribbons, or simply made into pigtails, I was apparently the cutest kid on the block.

I can hardly ever remember being reprimanded, refused anything or even prevented from doing exactly what I wanted to do. Looking back, I realise how bad this was for me. It not only made me selfish and rebellious, but also failed to teach me the value of anything that I had been given, and provided no boundaries. In my mind I was free to do as I pleased and very often did.

After a good first year at secondary school where I was amongst the top achievers in my class, the rest of my education was a complete shambles.

It all started when my class teacher, Mr Wilson, asked me at the start of my second year if I was the sister of Carmen Patterson. Carmen was three years older than me and had apparently caused some teachers grief during her first few years at school. If I had known then quite what was in store for me, I would have denied even knowing her!

However, after owning up to my older sibling, I was promptly told to wash out the classroom dustbins. I refused and was then given detention and told by Mr Wilson that as my sister Carmen reminded him of a monkey, so did I.

This sort of thing was still happening during the early 1980s when racism was hardly discussed in public, neither we nor our parents really knew how to confront it, and teachers were always right.

Mr Wilson continued to harass and embarrass me in front of the class and often referred to me and two of my black friends as the 'Three Wise Monkeys'. I told my mother how I was being treated but she didn't believe me, and when I reported it to the head teacher I was called 'a little liar' and given detention. It was then that I decided to take matters into my own hands.

My favourite television programme at the time was *Fantasy Island,* which featured voodoo and other forms of black magic. I was looking for something one day when a little black rag doll that belonged to one of my sisters fell from a cupboard. I took up the doll, then looked for the biggest needle I could find in my mother's sewing box and took them with me to school the next day.

I sat in my normal place, at the front of the class, and waited.

Mr Wilson, in his usual fashion, bawled me out for not having done my homework and then threatened me with detention.

I calmly took the doll from my bag and held it in front of me so that Mr Wilson could see it. I then began to 'stab' it with the needle, knowing that he was watching my every move. Suddenly, Mr Wilson started to sweat and a few minutes later he ran screaming from the classroom. He was away on sick leave for almost two months after that.

I was suspended for a few weeks but, having decided that school held little purpose for me anyway, truanted for two years.

During this time I met up with friends who were also truanting. We stayed at each other's houses whilst our parents were at work, went into town, had a few fights with pupils from neighbouring schools and took turns to shoplift.

It was not until the start of the fifth year that a teacher turned up at our house and asked about me. Of course, it was all too late then. Although I attended school for the last two months of the term, I left without any qualifications whatsoever.

On the very last day Mrs Johnson, one of the teachers who along with Mr Wilson had made my life hell, told me that I was only fit for the streets!

When I went on a YTS training course and worked in the medical centre of a local hospital, I earned £25 a week and loved it. At last, I felt like someone. People spoke kindly to me and a few even suggested that I should become a nurse. I was encouraged by the thought, but soon dismissed it. After all, I was uneducated and didn't have the confidence to learn. I was upset when I had to finish and really didn't care about the future.

The next few years were the worst in my life. I was done for grievous bodily harm for having beaten up my boyfriend's ex-girlfriend, took ecstasy as if it was going out of fashion and got pregnant at seventeen.

I was living at home, and after a few days of looking after my baby, Carla, I got fed up, gave her to my mother and went missing for several weeks. I couldn't stand the crying, the feeding, the winding – which I thought was stupid and didn't understand anyway – and the shitty nappies. Nobody knew where I was, and even though my sisters told me off for being so inconsiderate I still didn't care.

A few months later I got a flat in London and Carla and I went to live with her father, Danny. I found myself a job in a record shop, but the relationship between Danny and me broke up after a big fight that left me battered and bruised. I called my mother and a few days later I was back at home.

I later got a council house, and a job cleaning trains that I did for five years. I earned good money, but the shift hours made it difficult for me to look after Carla and so I left her with my parents, who were bringing her up as their own.

It wasn't long before I met up again with old friends, but this time I was a little older and wiser and refrained from the felonies that had been very much part of my life.

This had much to do with Finton. We met at a friend's party and he not only said how much he loved me but also treated me with respect. We moved in together after about four months and not long after this I got pregnant with my second child.

At last, my life was turning around. I felt good, confident, began to value myself more and started to enjoy being a mother. It was at this time that I wanted Carla back so that we could all be a family. She was nearly four years old and although I used to spend a lot of time with her, bought her things, and gave my parents money to look after her, I never told her that I was her mother until I went to collect her. It took a while before she could call me 'Mum' after having known me as 'Claudette', but it was even longer before she could call her sister, Jennifer, anything other than 'that baby'.

When I was made redundant from my cleaning job, I decided to learn to drive and passed first time. I then took a job as a Community Care worker at a residential home for elderly people. It meant a big drop in pay but the job was great. I loved the work and was good at it, and although many of the residents suffered from senile dementia, I was fascinated by the stories they had to tell.

My manager asked if I wanted to do a National Vocational Qualification Level 2 so that I could become a Senior Care Assistant, but I said no, because although I could read I didn't think I would be able to pass a test or even to take an exam.

Then one of my closest friends almost died of a drug overdose. I spent a lot of time with her, and when it appeared that she had recovered I had a call from her saying that she was admitting herself to the psychiatric hospital because she was afraid that she would harm herself if she stayed alone. When I said I would go with her, she said she didn't want me to see her in that way and didn't want me to visit. I was devastated.

Caring about my friend and for my patients, I became interested in mental health. It was then that the thought of becoming a Registered Mental Nurse came to me.

Being able to think of nothing else, I went straight away to the local college and signed up. When I told people that I was going to take a training course and go on to university, they laughed. No one thought I could succeed and I believed that no one wanted me to.

It was a struggle, and I had to do every assignment three times. The tutors were very helpful and supportive because they knew how hard I was trying. Six months into my course, people couldn't believe that I was still there, and at the end of the year I had achieved my Access to Nursing certificate and applied for a place at university.

I got an interview, and a place, and started my Diploma in Nursing course. I was ecstatic, my parents, children and sisters were all delighted for me and Finton – well, he apparently always knew that I had it in me.

But my personal happiness came to an abrupt end when I was called to the Dean's office a week after I had started my course. The police check had come back and the Dean wanted me to explain the police record that I had failed to declare on my registration form.

I was shattered and found it difficult to hold myself together. All I saw at that time was everything I had worked for just slipping away from me, and with it the best and only chance I had to make something of my life.

I could hardly speak but managed to say that I was a kid at the time and had put a girl in hospital for spreading lies about my family and me. I also managed to say that I hadn't declared it on my form because I had been told that after five years any criminal record you had would be obliterated.

I don't know whether it was how I looked or how I sounded that made the Dean say that she was prepared to give me a second chance, but she did. I thanked her and promised that I would work hard. I got myself to my little car and cried.

Being at university was a different world and it changed me. My attitude towards people was different; I became less judgemental and realised that things were not just black and white.

The assignments, reading and research were very hard, but I managed to do them because I took time out to read, and the more I read the more my grammar improved.

I used to go to bed late at night and was up and studying from about five in the morning. Sometimes things just would not sink in, and when I failed my Biology test twice I had to look for a different way of learning.

I photocopied and enlarged all the diagrams, labelled them and stuck them up on my bedroom wall. They were the last things I saw when I went to bed at night and the first things I saw when I woke up. After this I passed all my assignments, achieving A and B grades.

Whilst at university I worked for an agency to help make ends meet, and the children, seeing how hard I was trying, would read and do their homework without being nagged. I told them not to hang around too much with friends because they would hold them back.

My friends didn't benefit me. They made me into something bigger than I was – and that was really nothing. Most people feared me because I was horrible – school had made me horrible. I had no true friends; people only wanted to follow me because they thought I would stick up for them. I was no brains but all brawl.

Being at university and working seven days a week was a struggle. Finton provided when he could, as well as looking after the children, and I didn't spend above my means. If I had anything extra, I treated the children.

Each time I have changed my job I have taken a drop in pay, but my quest has never been about money, it has been about what I wanted to do and how I was going to achieve it. Some friends said that being on social security was a much easier life, but to me that would be no life at all.

In my last two months of training, I was on the ward nursing a patient called Mr Johnson. When his wife came to visit I saw it was my old teacher, Mrs Johnson, who had told me I was only fit for the streets. She asked if I remembered her but I pretended not to. She persisted, saying that she used to teach my sisters and me but I still didn't admit to knowing her. She then asked if I was a nurse and I said I was still training but that I had passed all my written exams and only had my final placements to complete. She then ended by saying that she had always thought I was a bright pupil and would make something of myself.

When I look back over my life, I am ashamed about some of the things I have done but I am a new person now, and having had five job offers, even before completing my training, I know that I have a worthwhile and valuable future ahead of me.

RHIANA'S STORY

My three older brothers and I grew up on a deprived council estate in Birmingham. Our parents were both manual workers and, although we were poor, we were happy.

My mother worked night shifts and I remember her coming home in the mornings, making our breakfast and getting us off to school. She would then go to sleep, but be up in time to cook dinner and to collect us. She left for work just as my father was coming in.

Although this went on for some years, money remained tight and so we never got everything we wanted, just what we needed. I didn't learn the difference between the two until I was older. The way my mother brought me up made me the woman I am today, because she really taught me how to juggle both emotional and financial situations.

Even though I was the youngest in the family, as the only other female I was expected to help my mother with the housework. So by my early teens I was pretty well versed in the domestic sphere. I could sew and I could cook and would clean the house from top to bottom. On Saturdays I would take two black bags of washing to the launderette and, believe it or not, this was an all day 'twin-tub' job.

I was eighteen before I had my first boyfriend, Trevor, who later became my husband, because I never really considered myself as being attractive. I had spots and wore glasses, but I always had a good figure and was proud of that. In fact, I can remember going from being flat-chested to a 36B in no time at all.

Trevor used to hang around with me and my best friend, Sheila, and I was surprised when he asked me to go out with him because I thought that he fancied her, especially as she was much prettier than me.

I wasn't interested at first because I saw Trevor as a playboy who was full of chat and just wanted to add me to the string of girlfriends that he already had. But he pursued me and eventually I gave in.

We had been going out together for about six months when I decided that I wanted to move to London. Things had started to get serious and, as I hadn't planned to settle down so soon, I wanted a chance to live by myself for a while. My parents were against the move, because they didn't think I was streetwise or worldly enough to live by myself and feared that I would either fall into bad company or get pregnant.

But going to London was the best thing I had ever done. I lived with Trevor's cousin in a flat in Hackney and worked for an agency before getting a full-time job as an office administrator.

Although we were still going out together, Trevor never came to see me in London, but we spent time together when I went back to see my parents.

Almost two years later, I moved back to Birmingham so that Trevor and I could get engaged. My parents didn't want us to get married because they didn't think he was good enough for me, but we decided to go ahead anyway.

We both worked and saved hard so that we could have the wedding we wanted without having to burden my parents, and then moved into a rented flat. Within two years we had bought our own home and our daughter, Lisa, was born.

Although we had good days when there would be no arguments, no atmosphere and some kind of emotional embrace, our marriage was far from being a happy one. Even from the start we hardly slept together. I would go up to bed and leave Trevor falling asleep on the sofa. He would say that he was coming up, but he rarely did, and after a while he only came to bed to have sex with me.

But it wasn't just the sex that made me feel cheap and worthless, it was also the fact that he took every opportunity there was to disparage me. When the telephone bills came in he would highlight the calls I had made, saying that I had to pay for them, and went on about me using the washing machine too often because of the size of the electricity bill.

Trevor continued with his 'put-downs' but I was able to cover things up so that no one knew what was going on. It became as easy as putting on make-up. But the cracks were beginning to show and I remember a friend telling me that once, when she heard him say something unpleasant to me, she was amazed that I didn't challenge him. It was then that I realised just how low I had sunk.

The physical abuse started two days after the christening of our second child, David, and it was over money.

I was on maternity leave at the time and, as my money had gone to cover the mortgage, this left very little for all the other things we needed. We had opened a bank account for our daughter and I decided that we should use some of the money we had saved in that account to get her a new coat. I had long suspected that Trevor had been taking money from the account and using it on himself, and when he became guarded and refused to hand over the bank book I knew that I was right.

A violent argument erupted, and I ran upstairs to use the phone in my bedroom to call my parents because I was afraid that he was going to hit me. After I left the room and was standing at the top of the stairs he came up behind and pushed me.

I remember holding on to the banister to stop myself falling, but I lost my footing and tumbled to the bottom of the stairs. When he came down after me I thought he was going to help me up but I was wrong. Instead he lifted me up by the neck and pinned me against the wall and threatened to kill me. I looked him straight in the eye and told him to do it. He wanted me to fight back so that he could have an excuse, and for that very reason I didn't. He later left the house.

The next few days it was like nothing at all had happened. Unable to contain myself I decided to tell him that he had gone too far. His callous response was that if he had, I would be dead. My parents came to see us because they were concerned about the situation and he apologised to them, but not to me.

He didn't hit me again for a long time, but made up for it with verbal and mental abuse. Things got so bad for me that one night I sat on the bed with a bottle of tranquillisers. As I was about to take them, my mobile phone rang. It was a friend and his comforting words saved me.

After that call I started to come to terms with how desperate my life had become and what I had to do to change it. Although we lived under the same roof, as far as I was concerned our marriage was over and so I started to live differently.

I had a good job as secretary to the chief executive of a major company and decided to focus on my career. I started by signing on to take a diploma in a business course, and with no support from Trevor had to ferry the children to and from my parents' between assignments. Whilst I took the chance to socialise more with friends from college and work, I also made sure that I kept on top of things at home so that Trevor had no excuse to pester me.

I was having a good time; I was growing, spreading my wings and learning how to value myself. Then it all came to an abrupt end when I refused to let Trevor touch me and swore at him for trying to do so.

He became violent, pushed me down onto the bed, straddled me and pinned each of my arms under his knees. I never fought him, and I remember thinking, God, please let me live.

When the rape was over, I simply told him that we were finished, that I had nothing more to say to him and that he would be hearing from my solicitor. I didn't have a solicitor and didn't really know what I was going to do. The only thing I was certain about, as I examined the bruises to my arms and face, was that I no longer wanted to live with this man.

A few days later I started legal proceedings and was told that if I were to leave the marital home I was likely to lose my children. The best thing I could do was to apply for an injunction that would enable us to continue living in the same house but would prevent him from abusing me. Although the injunction would cost me £500 and was only for three months, I decided to go for it. The morning when Trevor was served with the order he went berserk, but having told myself that I was not a victim, and that the law was there to protect me, I was no longer afraid of him and stood my ground.

But the vindictiveness continued and I remember one evening going into the kitchen to prepare supper. He was also in the kitchen and slowly picked up a knife and began to sharpen it. As I left the kitchen he placed the knife back on the draining board, only to pick it up again when I re-entered. This I knew was a message or a warning for me to watch myself. I stayed awake all that night because I knew how easy it would have been for him to kill me in my sleep.

After this, I did everything I could to avoid being alone with Trevor. If he was in a particular room in the house, I would simply go to another. Sometimes I would work at the office until well into the night, wander around the streets until it was late, or visit friends. At other times, if the children were with my parents and I could hear him moving around the house, I would get out of bed, dress myself and go into work. My office had become a safe haven for me.

Although I never once regretted the decision I had made, there were times when I felt that, if I had known how hard things were going to be, I would probably not have started the process.

With more legal wrangling my costs were mounting, and when Trevor decided to appeal against a further injunction and I was told that it would cost me £1500 to contest it, I decided that I would represent myself as I was the best person to tell my story.

My solicitor was good enough to instruct me in the process, advised me on how to address the judge and the approach my husband's lawyer was likely to take. I also went to the library and read through a few 'Guide to the Law' books so that I would be familiar with at least some of the legal jargon that would be used.

It was scary because I had never been in a situation like this before, but with the information I had gathered, and knowing what to expect, I was in a better position to present my case. I told myself that as long as I knew some of the rules I was more than capable of playing the game.

I stayed at my parents' house the night before the hearing, and it was only when Trevor turned up in court with his barrister, sister and a friend that I began to wish that I had brought someone with me. But it didn't matter in the end because the judge ruled in my favour.

Although I was strengthened by my efforts, after several months of mental abuse and tortuous manoeuvring, I decided to leave the house. I no longer felt safe there and, even though I risked losing my children by doing this, it was better for me to be alive for them.

It was two years before my divorce came through because Trevor contested it. He fought for the children and for the house. In the end I settled for less than half the property so that I could bring the matter to a close and we shared custody of the children. It was tough but I kept going and stayed focused on the end goal.

I never thought that I would be sitting in my own house and that I would be happy, but having achieved everything that I set out to achieve I am living my best years right now. My children are happier and, although it is not always easy for them to be in two separate houses, at least they are not seeing the two people they love trying to destroy each other.

Financially it has been hard going because although I continued to represent myself I am still in debt from the legal costs incurred from consulting with my solicitor.

The juggling I learned from my mother comes in handy, and if nothing else I now have a life that is worth living.

SUMMARY

Each of these stories demonstrates how we can choose not to be 'victims'. However difficult the challenges and what can appear to be impossible odds against us, we can always overcome. It would have been very easy for these two women to give up, as the odds were highly stacked against them, but instead of doing that they found inner strengths that allowed them to succeed.

Claudette's problems start as a result of simple prejudice. Because of a teacher's experience with her sister, it is assumed that she too will turn out to be difficult. Through no fault of her own she takes on the identity of troublemaker and, in doing so, reaffirms the prejudices. It is not until much later in her life that she recognises the need to change, and she does this by starting with herself. She develops a positive self-image and begins to believe that she has something to contribute. Next, she has to develop a strategy that allows others to start to believe in her. And she does this by demonstrating that she can achieve something.

Claudette shows she has the ability to exercise self-discipline, to work hard to apply herself. What she has done is to overcome adversity and in doing so she has quite literally re-invented herself. This is why many women, in a similar position, drastically change their hairstyles and the clothes they wear. It is confirmation, both to themselves and to others, that they have developed 'new' personalities.

Rhiana's story is an extreme case of a woman who has been subject to complete and utter humiliation over a number of years. Her self-confidence has been destroyed and she feels totally valueless. This is someone you would expect to escape into oblivion through drug or alcohol abuse. But she recognises that she has to keep going, for her own sake as well as for the children. She turns adversity into a virtue. She is convinced there is a better life and that, if only she can remain optimistic, she will be able to fulfil her lifelong dreams. Hers is a search for personal happiness.

SELF-HELP TIPS

- Respect yourself and maintain your positive self-esteem.

- Turn adversity to your advantage. In working out solutions to problems, you will create a long-term strategic way of thinking which is vital for your personal success.

- Prove to others that *you can do it*. This is best demonstrated by studying for professional and educational qualifications. This will show your stamina and your ability to exercise self-discipline and work hard.

- Demonstrate the capacity for self-reinvention.

- Never allow the opinion of others to shape your own sense of self-worth. Through overcoming adversity, you will develop self-confidence and the ability to be assertive.

IN THE CORPORATION

There are always ups and downs in the modern corporation. We get passed over for promotion. We lose our jobs. Our appraisers and/or line managers do not think that we are up to the job. In short, our working lives are full of traumas and disappointments.

The corporate high-flyers are the people who can handle all of these setbacks. They refuse to be defeated. They never see themselves as victims. They will absorb anything that is thrown at them and turn it to their own advantage. Humiliation and defeat are words that do not exist in their vocabularies.

Indeed, these experiences give them resilience, resoluteness and determination, and make them even tougher – not weaker. It is why so many entrepreneurs originate from deprived or disadvantaged backgrounds. They have had to overcome every bit of adversity, and this has given them the personal qualities vital for business success.

And so it is in the modern corporation. To be successful, you have to be tough. Not in the sense of how you treat other people, but in the sense of being self-assured, self-confident and with an unfaltering belief in yourself. Above all else, these are the attributes of those who climb the corporate ladder, break through all the barriers and gain access to their well-deserved seat at the boardroom table.

Afterword

All of the women described in this book have been through traumatic experiences. Some of these have been frightening and even life-threatening. But every one of them has turned these to their own advantage. At the end of the day, they are all winners.

We live in a world of qualifications. Big business insists on pieces of paper to determine whether people are available for filling vacant positions. We are profiled in terms of our intellectual, emotional and social intelligence. Do we have the brains and the ability to do the job? Can we cope with stress and the pressures of work? And, finally, are we able to work with other people in teams and to serve the interests of the company? But it goes even further than this.

From a very early age, the school system prepares us for the world of work. We are tested from the age of eleven and this continues through until we are sixteen. If we carry on to college and university, the testing continues until we are in our early twenties. Even then, it is often not enough. Companies now expect us to have MBAs to ensure that we have the abilities to cope with modern corporate life.

But since when has business life been dependent upon formal qualifications? How far does the rote learning of management text-books prepare us for the tensions and problems of everyday work? Is the analysis of case studies sufficient preparation for the consequential decisions that we have to take as managers, colleagues and team leaders? In our view, not a lot. Certainly, not in comparison with how life experiences can equip us with more effective business skills. The stories in this book demonstrate forcefully this very point.

Big business is now in crisis. Customers no longer trust or believe the advertisements. Employees are increasingly suspicious of the motives of their bosses. They have seen how the 'fat cats' get rewarded for failure while, at the same time, the value of their own pensions has gone down the tubes. The natural reaction for many is to 'follow the leader' and to get away with doing as little as possible. No wonder employee morale in large businesses is at rock bottom.

It is hardly surprising that young people do not want to work in large companies any more. They have seen what these businesses have done to their parents. For many, it was twenty or thirty years of dedicated service followed by redundancy and long unemployment after that recent takeover bid.

More people want to go it alone and set up their own businesses. The attractions of entrepreneurship have never been greater. Why? Because men and women are more cynical about the ways they are being treated by their employers. For women, it is almost an everyday story of how they get passed over for promotion. The usual explanation by the personnel department is lack of qualifications for the job. 'You are a great person doing a great job, but you don't have the qualifications to be promoted to the next grade.' And so, in response, more women are quitting their jobs and setting up their own businesses. Good luck to them, but what a waste of talent for large companies – and solely because of their own blinkered-eyes, closed-minds and blocked-ears approach to staff development.

The women described in this book have done it the hard way. Out of their experiences, they have developed skills in financial management, strategy, team-building, time management, decision-making and handling crises. What more do companies want? But our guess is that, if many of them applied for jobs through the normal form-filling channels, their applications would be turned down.

But things are changing. There is no question that many of the women in this book could successfully run their own businesses. But what is also good about the growth of the small firm sector is that these businesses are likely to be far more open-minded than larger companies. They appreciate that paper qualifications are not the 'be all and end all'. What they are looking for are people with a positive attitude who are prepared to tackle and overcome major challenges. In other words, people of the kind described in this book.

Over the next decade, Britain will face major skill shortages. It can no longer afford to overlook the talents and the skills that are not fully utilised because they are hidden among men and women without formal qualifications. It will be necessary for companies to remove the blinkers from their eyes, to open up their closed minds and to unblock their ears. They will have to develop far more imaginative approaches to staff selection. They will have to shift away from their obsession with profiling, psychological testing and paper qualifications. Instead, they will need to experiment with new techniques of recruitment. In this, they will have to take a look at how small firms do it. Many high-performing small companies 'take a chance', 'stick their necks out' and, generally speaking, take risks in their recruitment policies. This is why they are entrepreneurial and why they often get the best out of their staff.

The women in this book possess huge reserves of talent and determination. It will be a great loss to the British economy if strategies are not developed by companies to embrace and capitalise upon these. But, equally, it will be a great shame if women themselves fail to recognise what they have to offer. The problem for many women is that they lack self-confidence and, with this, self-respect. As the stories in this book describe, these circumstances are so often quite literally knocked out of them by their male partners. They encounter experiences in their lives so that they feel undermined and with little self-worth. It is imperative that these women cease to see themselves as victims. That they recognise the strengths which they possess and they build upon these in order to rebuild their self-esteem. The stories in this book describe how this can be done. We live in a world where everyone is battling for themselves. It is a pity is so but that is the reality of life. Of course, there are counselling services and a broad range of support systems available for those in desperate need. But, in the final analysis, it is up to ourselves. By overcoming adversity, it is possible for women to develop the capabilities not only to become self-confident but also to acquire the skills to walk from the kitchen sink to the boardroom table.

Richard Scase

OTHER BLACKAMBER TITLES

The Demented Dance
Mounsi

The Cardamom Club
Jon Stock

Something Black in the Lentil Soup
Reshma S. Ruia

Typhoon
The Holy Woman
Qaisra Shahraz

Ma
All That Blue
Gaston-Paul Effa

Paddy Indian
The Uncoupling
Cauvery Madhavan

Foreday Morning
Paul Dash

Ancestors
Paul Crooks

Nothing but the Truth
Mark Wray

Hidden Lights
Joan Blaney

What Goes Around
Sylvester Young

Brixton Rock
Alex Wheatle

One Bright Child
Patricia Cumper

All BlackAmber books are available from your local bookshop.

For a regular update on BlackAmber' latest release, with extracts, reviews and events, visit:

www.blackamber.com